SEEDLIP
COCKTAILS

SEEDLIP
COCKTAILS

100 DELICIOUS
NONALCOHOLIC RECIPES
FROM SEEDLIP &
THE WORLD'S BEST BARS

weldon**owen**

WELDON OWEN
1150 Brickyard Cove Road
Richmond, CA 94801
www.weldonowen.com

weldon**owen**

First published in 2018 by Bantam Press, an imprint of Transworld.
Transworld is part of the Penguin Random House group of companies.

ISBN 978-1-68188-510-0

Designed and typeset in Brown & Baskerville/11pt by Smith & Gilmour
Printed and bound in China by C&C Offset Printing Co., Ltd.

3 5 7 9 10 8 6 4

CONTENTS

WHAT IS SEEDLIP?

Seedlip is a nature company on a mission to change the way the world drinks by solving the *what to drink when you're not drinking* dilemma with the world's first distilled nonalcoholic spirits.

Served in the best restaurants, bars & hotels in the world, Seedlip is inspired by Ben Branson's family's 300-year farming heritage & *The Art of Distillation*, a book written in 1651 detailing the distilled nonalcoholic herbal remedies produced by apothecaries.

The three Seedlip spirits – Spice 94, Garden 108 & Grove 42 – are blended & bottled in England. Seedlip has created a bespoke maceration, copper pot distillation & filtration process for each plant to capture & celebrate the true flavors of nature. All three Seedlip spirits are free from not only alcohol, but also sugar, sweeteners, calories & allergens, making them the ideal grown-up option if you're not drinking – whatever the reason.

WELCOME

Thank you for buying *Seedlip Cocktails*.

We launched Seedlip back in November 2015. I'd been working on Seedlip for over two years, bringing together things I'm passionate about – nature, farming, design & ingredients – into a bottle. I knew that the *what to drink when you're not drinking* dilemma needed solving & hoped others would share my view that it was time for the world of nonalcoholic drinks to be taken seriously. Thankfully, I have since come across so many wonderful people who share that vision & who are helping us to change the way the world drinks.

This book is a celebration of nature through some of our favorite recipes & recipes from some of the world's best bartenders. It's not for your coffee table; it's for folded corners, scribbles, tatty pages & Post-its. There are simple recipes & simple techniques; really fiddly recipes & some really unusual gadgets[1]; everyday, ordinary ingredients & forgotten, rare ones, too.

Whether you're a professional bartender or an at-home experimenter, I hope these pages demonstrate that cocktails without alcohol, when taken seriously, can be both delicious & a lot of fun[2].

Peas & love

Ben

---

[1] Do refer to the glossary at the back when in doubt!
[2] The guest recipes are trickier. They highlight just how creative we've been getting with Seedlip & offer an opportunity for more experienced bartenders to experiment!

FIVE FACTS ABOUT SEEDLIP

1

A seedlip is a seed sower's basket. Seedlips were used
by Ben's family over 300 years ago to hand-sow seed.

2

Carolus Linnaeus – "the godfather of botany" – gave 4,000
animals their Latin names, including the fox, the hare & the
squirrel that feature on the front of Seedlip's bottles.

3

Some of Ben's ancestors' initials are hidden in the fox
illustration on Spice 94.

4

Seedlip is the proud owner of a copy of *The Art of Distillation*
that dates back to 1664. The original copy can
be found in the British Library & used to belong
to King George III.

5

The first 1,000 bottles of Seedlip sold out in 3 weeks,
the second in 3 days & the third in just 30 minutes.

OUR APPROACH TO COCKTAILS

In bars, restaurants & hotels, the backbars brim with alcoholic options. And there are hundreds of years of tried & tested recipes using these ingredients. So, with a wealth of books, websites & home barware to experiment with, it has never been easier to have a go at home.

However, proper nonalcoholic cocktails are new. There aren't lots of products, recipes & information. And this is what makes it so exciting. The limitations – creativity's greatest ally – are actually very liberating. There are no established "ways" to make nonalcoholic cocktails; there aren't any "classics" yet; there have not been 100 years of "this is how it must be made." Instead, there is an opportunity to create the classic Seedlip cocktails of the future.

We like to approach each Seedlip cocktail as a chef approaches a plate of food, pairing great ingredients in interesting ways to produce fantastic flavors. The three distinct flavor profiles of Spice 94, Garden 108 & Grove 42 complement different plants & different combinations. Once we have a combination in mind (for example, Spice 94 with ginger & cashew, or Garden 108 with basil & strawberry), we can then explore the best techniques, the right quantities, the ideal glassware, what kind of ice, what garnish &, of course, what we're going to call it!

INGREDIENTS & PAIRINGS

*Here are some examples of ingredients & food pairings that work
particularly well with each of the three Seedlip flavors.*

SPICE 94

Complementary Ingredients: Grapefruit, Pineapple,
Vanilla, Maple, Cinnamon, Coffee
Can be paired with: Red Meat, Root Veg, Curries, Desserts, Petits Fours

GARDEN 108

Complementary Ingredients: Apple, Rhubarb,
Basil, Cucumber, Elderflower, Lime
Can be paired with: Starters, White Fish, Salads, Palate Cleansers, Sorbets

GROVE 42

Complementary Ingredients: Peanut, Carrot,
Barley, Ginger, Honey, Apricot
Can be paired with: Pâté, Spicy Dishes, Shellfish, Game, Chocolate-Based Desserts

THE EIGHT TENETS FOR NONALCOHOLIC COCKTAILS

Here are some principles we abide by when creating drinks.

1
G.I.G. [GLASS. ICE. GARNISH.]
Smart glass, lots of ice
& don't forget the garnish.

2
THINK LIKE A CHEF
Think flavor & ingredients first,
then the delivery.

3
REUSE, REDUCE, RECYCLE
Syrups, shrubs, ferments, jams
& salts are all handy ways to reduce
your waste & add a real depth of flavor
to nonalcoholic cocktails.
Make sure to reuse produce or
recycle ingredients.

4
STAY SEASONAL (WHERE POSSIBLE)
Being in tune with the rhythm
of the seasons & your climate feels
better, tastes better & is better
for the environment.

5
STAY LOCAL (WHERE POSSIBLE)
Find your local farm shop or
"pick-your-own" farm, grow your own
or check out some of the amazing fruit
& veg box services available.

6
"ROOT TO SHOOT"
We're all familiar with nose to tail
or farm to table; "root to shoot" is our
Seedlip equivalent. The stone, the peel,
the leaves, the flowers – all are tasty
in their own right.

7
HOST WITH THE MOST
One of the most powerful ways to
delight guests & truly be the perfect host
is to prioritize your guests' experience &
consider their individual requirements.
Whether that means taking into
account someone's allergy or that
someone is driving or vegetarian –
leave no one out.

8
NO MOCKING
The word *mocktails* is an insult! Let's talk about *Seedlip
cocktails* or *nonalcoholic cocktails* instead. Please.

PROFILE

Aromatic & Complex

PLANTS

Allspice Berries
Green Cardamom
Oak
Cascarilla Bark
Grapefruit Peel
Lemon Peel

FREE FROM

Sugar
Sweeteners
Common Allergens

SEEDLIP

—

SPICE 94

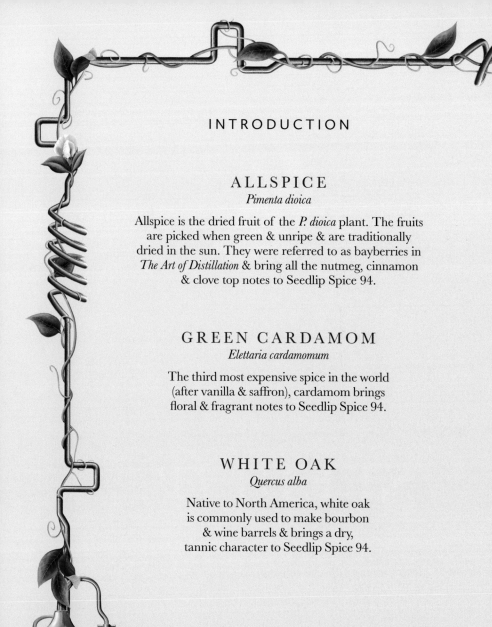

INTRODUCTION

ALLSPICE
Pimenta dioica

Allspice is the dried fruit of the *P. dioica* plant. The fruits
are picked when green & unripe & are traditionally
dried in the sun. They were referred to as bayberries in
The Art of Distillation & bring all the nutmeg, cinnamon
& clove top notes to Seedlip Spice 94.

GREEN CARDAMOM
Elettaria cardamomum

The third most expensive spice in the world
(after vanilla & saffron), cardamom brings
floral & fragrant notes to Seedlip Spice 94.

WHITE OAK
Quercus alba

Native to North America, white oak
is commonly used to make bourbon
& wine barrels & brings a dry,
tannic character to Seedlip Spice 94.

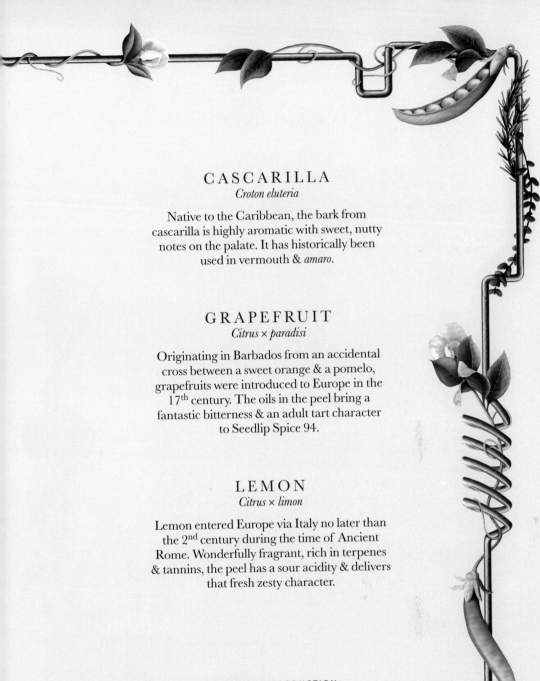

CASCARILLA
Croton eluteria

Native to the Caribbean, the bark from cascarilla is highly aromatic with sweet, nutty notes on the palate. It has historically been used in vermouth & *amaro*.

GRAPEFRUIT
Citrus × paradisi

Originating in Barbados from an accidental cross between a sweet orange & a pomelo, grapefruits were introduced to Europe in the 17th century. The oils in the peel bring a fantastic bitterness & an adult tart character to Seedlip Spice 94.

LEMON
Citrus × limon

Lemon entered Europe via Italy no later than the 2nd century during the time of Ancient Rome. Wonderfully fragrant, rich in terpenes & tannins, the peel has a sour acidity & delivers that fresh zesty character.

MENU

LONG COCKTAILS

SPICE & GINGER
ALL THE SPICE
ELIZA
SPICE BOOCH
VANILLA
PUMPKIN
PINEAPPLE

SHORT COCKTAILS

NODDY
ESPRESSO MARTI**NO**
SPICE MARTI**NO**
MR HOWARD
NOGRONI

SPICE 94
LONG COCKTAILS · SHORT COCKTAILS

CHAPTER
1

SPICE & GINGER

—

The ancient Greeks ate ginger wrapped in bread. They eventually decided to add ginger to the bread & gingerbread was born.

INGREDIENTS

—

Spice 94: 2 oz
Fever-Tree Ginger Ale: Top
Ice: Cubed
Garnish: Lime Wedge
Glass: Tall

METHOD

—

Fill a tall glass with ice

Add Spice 94

Top with ginger ale

Garnish with a lime wedge

ALL THE SPICE

SPICE 94 · TONIC/SODA · GRAPEFRUIT

—

Christopher Columbus came across allspice berries in Jamaica in 1494.

INGREDIENTS

—

Spice 94: 2 oz
Tonic/Soda: Top
Ice: Cubed
Garnish: Grapefruit Twist
Glass: Tall

METHOD

—

Fill a tall glass with ice

Add Spice 94

Top with tonic or soda

Garnish with a grapefruit twist

ELIZA

SPICE 94 · MARMALADE · CASSIA

—

This recipe is a tribute to Madam Eliza Cholmondeley, whose 1677 recipe book featured one of the earliest marmalade recipes.

INGREDIENTS

—

Spice 94: 2 oz
Marmalade: 1 tsp
Soda: Top
Ice: Cubed
Garnish: Charred Cassia Bark
Glass: Jam Jar

METHOD

—

Add Spice 94 & marmalade to a shaker with ice

Shake for 30 seconds

Strain into a jam jar

Top with soda

To char the cassia bark, light the end until it begins to smoke

Garnish with charred cassia bark

SPICE BOOCH

SPICE 94 · KOMBUCHA · LEMON

—

Kombucha has 80 other names worldwide, including Zaubertrank, which is German for "magic potion."

INGREDIENTS
—

Spice 94: 2 oz
Kombucha (*see page 186*): Top
Ice: Cubed
Garnish: Lemon Twist
Glass: Tumbler

METHOD
—

Fill a tumbler with ice

Add Spice 94

Top with Kombucha

Garnish with a lemon twist

VANILLA

—

*According to popular belief, the Totonac people from the
east coast of Mexico were the first to cultivate vanilla.*

INGREDIENTS
—

Spice 94: 2 oz
Vanilla Extract: 1 tsp
Soda: Top
Ice: Cubed
Garnish: Green Apple Slice
Glass: Tumbler

METHOD
—

Fill a tumbler with ice

Add Spice 94 & vanilla extract

Top with soda

Garnish with a slice of green apple

PUMPKIN

SPICE 94 · GINGER · PUMPKIN · LEMON

—

Pumpkins are actually a fruit from the Cucurbitaceae family.
Other members include cucumbers & certain melons.

INGREDIENTS

—

Spice 94: 2 oz
Ginger & Pumpkin Shrub (*see page 64*): 1 oz
Soda: Top
Ice: Cut Block
Garnish: Lemon Twist
Glass: Tall

METHOD

—

Fill a tall glass with ice

Add Spice 94 & Ginger & Pumpkin Shrub & stir

Top with soda

Garnish with a lemon twist

PINEAPPLE

SPICE 94 · LIME · PINEAPPLE · SAGE

—

It can take up to 3 years for a single pineapple to mature &, once harvested, it stops ripening.

INGREDIENTS

—

Spice 94: 2 oz
Fresh Lime Juice: 1 tsp
Pineapple Tepache (*see page 67*): 2 ¼ oz
Ice: Cubed
Garnish: Sage Leaf
Glass: Tumbler

METHOD

—

Fill a tumbler with ice

Add Spice 94 & lime juice

Top with Pineapple Tepache

Garnish with a sage leaf

NODDY

SPICE 94 · LEMON · HONEY

—

January 11th is National Hot Toddy Day &
June 21st is International Gnome Day.

INGREDIENTS

—

Spice 94: 2 oz
Fresh Lemon Juice: 1 tbsp
Manuka Honey: 1 tbsp
Boiling Water: Top
Garnish: Lemon Wheel
Glass: Mug

METHOD

—

Add Spice 94, lemon juice & honey to a mug

Top with boiling water & stir

Garnish with a lemon wheel

ESPRESSO MARTI**NO**

—

A young goat herder first discovered coffee in Ethiopia circa AD*800.*

INGREDIENTS
—

Spice 94: 2 oz
Sandows Cold Brew Concentrate (*see page 186*): 2 oz
Sugar Syrup (*see page 186*): 1 tbsp
Ice: Cubed
Garnish: 3 Coffee Beans
Glass: Coupe

METHOD
—

Add Spice 94, Sandows Cold Brew Concentrate
& Sugar Syrup to a shaker

Add ice & shake

Double strain into a coupe glass

Garnish with 3 coffee beans

SPICE MARTI**NO**

—

Verjus is the juice of unripe white grapes. The word derives
from the middle French vert jus, meaning "green juice."

INGREDIENTS

—

Spice 94: 2 oz
Verjus (White Grape Juice): 2 tsp
Olive Brine: 1 tsp
Ice: Cubed
Garnish: Nocellara Olive
Glass: Coupe

METHOD

—

Add ice to a mixing glass with the Spice 94,
verjus & olive brine

Stir for 45 seconds

Strain into a coupe glass

Garnish with a Nocellara olive

MR HOWARD

SPICE 94 · GRAPEFRUIT · LEMON · STAR ANISE

—

This cocktail is named after Stewart Howard,
one of the first people in the world to serve Seedlip.

INGREDIENTS

—

Spice 94: 2 oz
Fresh Pink Grapefruit Juice: 1 oz
Fresh Lemon Juice: 1 tbsp
Sugar Syrup (*see page 186*): 1 tbsp
Ice: Cubed
Garnish: Star Anise
Glass: Coupe

METHOD

—

Add Spice 94, grapefruit juice, lemon juice
& sugar syrup to a shaker with ice

Shake for 30 seconds

Double strain into a coupe glass

Garnish with a star anise

NOGRONI®

SPICE 94 · BITTER · SWEET

———

*This drink was born in Ben Branson's garage & debuted
at the World's 50 Best Bar Awards in London in 2017.*

INGREDIENTS

———

Spice 94: 1 oz
Nonalcoholic Bitter Aperitif (*see page 64*): 1 oz
Nonalcoholic Sweet Vermouth (*see page 64*): 1 oz
Ice: Cut Block
Garnish: Orange Twist
Glass: Tumbler

METHOD

———

Add ice to a tumbler

Pour in the Spice 94, Bitter Aperitif & Sweet Vermouth

Stir for 20 seconds

Garnish with an orange twist

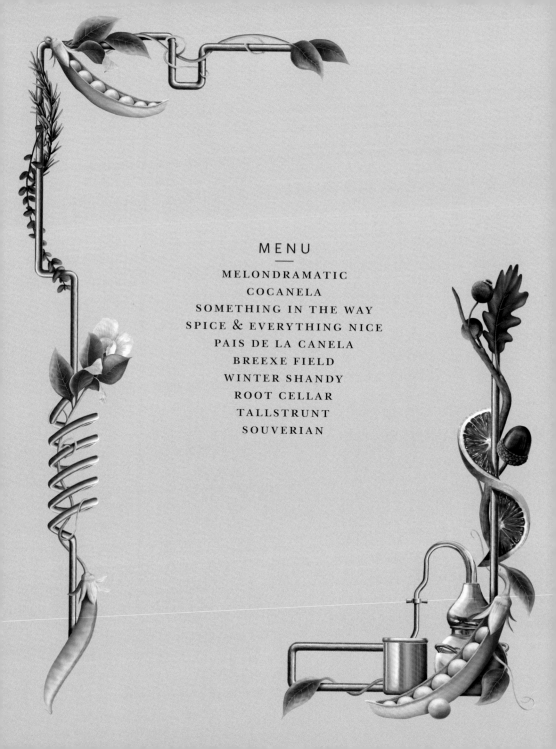

MENU

—

MELONDRAMATIC

COCANELA

SOMETHING IN THE WAY

SPICE & EVERYTHING NICE

PAIS DE LA CANELA

BREEXE FIELD

WINTER SHANDY

ROOT CELLAR

TALLSTRUNT

SOUVERIAN

SPICE 94

GUEST COCKTAILS

A selection of cocktails from some of the world's best bartenders

CHAPTER

2

MELONDRAMATIC

SPICE 94 · KOLA · WATERMELON · LEMON MYRTLE

—

MICHAEL CHIEM & THOR BERGQUIST– PS40, SYDNEY
Cocktail Bar of the Year 2018 – Time Out Australia

INGREDIENTS
—

Spice 94: 2 oz
Kola Nut Tea (*see page 64*): 1 oz
Rectified Watermelon Juice (*see page 65*): 1 oz
PS Lemon Myrtle Soda (*see page 186*): 2 oz
Ice: Cubed
Garnish: Watermelon Ball & Watermelon Rind Dust
Glass: Tumbler

METHOD
—

Add all the ingredients to a tumbler over ice

Garnish with a watermelon ball

Toast the skin of the watermelon with a blowtorch,
then grate the toasted part over the top

COCANELA

SPICE 94 · COCONUT · HONEY · LEMON · CINNAMON

—

DEV JOHNSON – EMPLOYEES ONLY, NEW YORK CITY

37th Best Bar in the World – World's 50 Best Bar Awards 2017

INGREDIENTS

—

Spice 94: 2 oz
Coconut Milk: 1 oz
Honey Syrup (*see page 185*): 1 tbsp
Fresh Lemon Juice: 1 tbsp
Sugar Syrup (*see page 186*): 1 tbsp
Ice: Crushed
Garnish: Grated Cinnamon
Glass: Tall

METHOD

—

Add all the ingredients to a tall glass & fill with crushed ice

Gently mix with a barspoon

Grate cinnamon over the top to garnish

SOMETHING
IN THE WAY

SPICE 94 · FAUX VERMOUTH · MAPLE

—

ROBIN GOODFELLOW – PRETTY UGLY & BAR RAVAL, TORONTO

Both bars were Top 10 Canada Cocktail Bars 2018 – Canada's 100 Best Bar & Restaurant Awards

INGREDIENTS
—
Spice 94: 1 ½ oz
Maple Faux Vermouth (*see page 65*): 1 ½ oz
Ice: Large Cut Clear Block
Garnish: Maple Leaf
Glass: Tumbler

METHOD
—

Add all the ingredients to a tumbler

Garnish with a maple leaf

SPICE &
EVERYTHING NICE

SPICE 94 · CHAMOMILE · PINK PEPPERCORN · PEAR

—

NICOLAS TORRES – LAZY BEAR, SAN FRANCISCO

2 Michelin Stars – Michelin Guide 2017

INGREDIENTS

—

Spice 94: 1 ½ oz
Heavy-Steeped Chamomile Tea: 1 oz
Pink Peppercorn Gum Syrup (*see page 186*): 1 tbsp
D'Anjou Pear Vinegar (*see page 184*): 2 tsp
Fee Bros Nonalcoholic Aromatic Bitters (*see page 184*): 4 dashes
Ice: Cubed
Garnish (optional): Lemon Peel
Glass: Coupe

METHOD

—

Add all the ingredients to a mixing glass & stir

Strain into a coupe glass

Garnish with a lemon peel (optional)

PAIS DE LA CANELA

SPICE 94 · CELERY · CINNAMON · GRAPEFRUIT

—

AIDAN BOWIE – THE AVIARY, CHICAGO
41ˢᵗ Best Bar in the World – World's 50 Best Bar Awards 2017

INGREDIENTS
—

Spice 94: 1 ½ oz
Celery Root & Cinnamon Cordial (*see page 65*): ¾ oz
Cider Spice Noir Tea: 1 oz
Apple Cider Vinegar: 2 dashes
Ice: Cut Block
Garnish: Grapefruit Zest
Glass: Tumbler

METHOD
—

Add all the ingredients to a mixing glass & stir

Strain over a rock of ice into a tumbler

Garnish with grapefruit zest

BREEZE FIELD
SPICE 94 · ORANGE · PROVENCE · SAFFRON

—

GIACOMO GIANNOTTI – PARADISO, BARCELONA
36th Best Bar in the World – World's 50 Best Bar Awards 2017

INGREDIENTS
—

Spice 94: 2 oz
Rectified Orange Juice (*see page 66*): ½ oz
Bitter Orange Marmalade: 1 barspoon
Bitter Syrup (*see page 184*): 1 tsp
Lemon & Ginger Juice (*see page 185*): 1 tbsp
Saffron Essence: 1 dash
Ice: Cubed
Garnish: Orange Twist & Lemon Thyme Sprig
Glass: Champagne Flute

METHOD
—

Add all the ingredients to a shaker with ice & shake

Strain into a Champagne flute

Garnish with an orange twist & a sprig of lemon thyme

WINTER SHANDY

SPICE 94 · APRICOT · LEMON · MALT · NUTMEG

—

JOSH HARRIS – TRICK DOG, SAN FRANCISCO
26ᵗʰ Best Bar in the World – World's 50 Best Bar Awards 2017

INGREDIENTS

—

Spice 94: 2 oz
Spiced Apricot Ceylon Shrub (*see page 66*): 1 oz
Fresh Lemon Juice: 2 tsp
Sugar Syrup (*see page 186*): 1 barspoon
Erdinger Nonalcoholic Beer: 3 oz
Ice: Cubed
Garnish: Grapefruit Zest & Peel & Grated Nutmeg
Glass: Tumbler

METHOD

—

Add all the ingredients except
the Erdinger to a shaker

Add the ice & shake

Double strain into a tumbler

Add fresh cubes of ice & top with Erdinger

Garnish with grapefruit zest & peel,
then grate nutmeg over the top

ROOT CELLAR
SPICE 94 · CELERY ROOT · CELERY
—

ANYA MONTAGUE – BLUE HILL AT STONE BARNS, NEW YORK
12th Best Restaurant in the World – World's 50 Best Restaurant Awards 2018

INGREDIENTS
—
Spice 94: 1 ½ oz
Celery Root Tincture (*see page 66*): 1 tsp
Celery Root Syrup (*see page 66*): 1 tsp
Celery Seed Salt Solution (*see page 184*): 3 drops
Verjus (White Grape Juice): 2 tsp
Pu'erh Tea (*see page 186*): 2 tsp
Ice: Cut Block
Garnish: Celery Leaf
Glass: Tumbler

METHOD
—
Add all the ingredients to a tumbler

Garnish with a celery leaf

TALLSTRUNT

SPICE 94 · CLOUDBERRY · PINE

—

JIMMIE HULTH – LINJE TIO, STOCKHOLM

44th Best Bar in the World – World's 50 Best Bar Awards 2017

INGREDIENTS
—

Spice 94: 2 oz
Cloudberry Cordial (*see page 67*): 1 tbsp
Pine Tree Syrup (*see page 67*): 2 tsp
Apple Cider Vinegar: 2 dashes
Ice: Cubed
Garnish: Spruce Sprig
Glass: Tumbler

METHOD
—

Add all the ingredients to a tumber filled with ice

Garnish with a sprig of spruce

SOUVERIAN

SPICE 94 · VERJUS · PEACH · GINGER

—

DEVON TARBY – THE WALKER INN, LOS ANGELES

World Top 100 Bar – World's Best Bar Awards 2017

INGREDIENTS
—
Spice 94: 1 ½ oz
Verjus (White Grape Juice): 1 tbsp
Fresh Lemon Juice: 1 tbsp
Spiced Peach Cordial (*see page 67*): ¾ oz
Ginger Syrup: 1 tsp
Ice: Pebble & Cubed
Garnish: Mint Leaf & Lemon Wheel
Glass: Tumbler

METHOD
—
Add the ingredients to a mixing glass with a small
amount of pebble ice & whip until the ice dissolves

Pour into a tumbler & add ice cubes

Cover with a second glass & shake

Strain into a tumbler over fresh ice

Garnish with a mint leaf & a lemon wheel

GINGER & PUMPKIN SHRUB

MAKES APPROX. 2 CUPS

—

INGREDIENTS

Fresh Root Ginger: 5 oz
Pumpkin: 14 oz
Cider Vinegar: 1 cup
Superfine Sugar: 1 ¼ cups

METHOD

Peel & grate the ginger. Peel, seed &
roughly chop the pumpkin. Add all the
ingredients to a Mason jar & muddle. Leave
for 24 hours in the fridge. Fine strain & bottle.
Keeps refrigerated for 1 month

NONALCOHOLIC
BITTER APERITIF

MAKES 2 CUPS

—

INGREDIENTS

Fabri Bitter Syrup *(see page 184)*: ⅔ cup
Monin Bitter Syrup *(see page 184)*: ⅔ cup
Citric Tea (orange & pink grapefruit
peel soaked in boiling water for 1 hour,
then strained): ¼ cup
Wormwood Tea (wormwood chippings
soaked in boiling water for
1 hour, then strained): ⅓ cup
Fruit Tea (Chamomile Tea, Vanilla
Black Tea, Bouquet Garni Tea &
Ground Mixed Spice soaked in boiling
water for 1 hour, then strained): ⅔ cup

METHOD

Add all the ingredients together
& stir well. Store in glass bottles.
Keeps for 1 month

NONALCOHOLIC SWEET
VERMOUTH

MAKES APPROX. 1 QUART

—

INGREDIENTS

Verjus (White Grape Juice): 2 cups
Sweet & Dandy *(see page 186)*: 1 cup
Sorrel Juice *(see page 186)*: 1 cup
Tonka Bean Droplets *(see page 187)*: 38
Oak Smoke Droplets *(see page 185)*: 38
Vanilla Extract: 1 tsp
Caramel Syrup: 2 tbsp
Tartaric Acid *(see page 186)*: 1 tsp
Pink Grapefruit Peel: 1–2
Orange Peel: 1–2

METHOD

Add all the ingredients to a
container & stir well. Refrigerate
for 5 hours. Fine strain & bottle.
Keeps refrigerated for 3 weeks

KOLA NUT TEA

MAKES APPROX. 1 ⅔ CUPS

—

INGREDIENTS

Water: 1 ¼ cups
Powdered Kola Nut *(see page 186)*: ¼ cup
Cane Sugar: 1 ½ cups

METHOD

Add the water & kola nut to a saucepan
& bring to a boil. Remove from the heat
& add the sugar, stirring to dissolve.
Cover & leave for 20 minutes.
Fine strain & bottle.
Keeps for 1 month

RECTIFIED WATERMELON JUICE

MAKES 2 CUPS

—

INGREDIENTS

Watermelon Juice: 2 cups
Citric Acid: 5 tsp
Malic Acid: 1 tbsp
Salt: Pinch

METHOD

Fine strain the watermelon juice into
a bowl. Add all the other ingredients
& stir, then bottle.
Keeps refrigerated for 1 week

CELERY ROOT & CINNAMON CORDIAL

MAKES APPROX. 1 ⅔ CUPS

—

INGREDIENTS

Celery Stick: 1
Salt: Pinch
Cinnamon Sticks: 1 oz
Superfine Sugar: 1 ¼ cups

METHOD

Cut the celery into chunks & put through
a juicer. Measure 2 cups of the celery
juice into a saucepan over medium heat
& reduce by half. Add the salt & stir.
Remove from the heat, add the
cinnamon & sugar
& stir to dissolve. Leave to cool.
Strain & bottle.
Keeps refrigerated for 3 weeks

MAPLE FAUX VERMOUTH

MAKES APPROX. 1 GALLON

—

INGREDIENTS

Water: 10 quarts
Grapefruit: 2
Lemons: 3
Anise Seeds: 2
Coriander Seeds: 1 tsp
Pink Peppercorns: 1 tsp
Dried Lemongrass: 1 tsp
Dried Osmanthus Flower: 2 tsp
Dried Honeysuckle: 1 tsp
Gentian: ½ tsp
Wormwood: ½ tsp
Dried Fir Tips: 2 tsp
Maple Syrup: ⅞ cup

METHOD

Put the water into a saucepan & bring to
a boil. Zest the grapefruits & lemons &
add to the pan with all the other
ingredients, except the maple syrup.
Reduce the heat & simmer until the
liquid has reduced to 3 ½ quarts. Strain,
add the maple syrup to sweeten
& bottle.
Keeps refrigerated for 2 weeks

RECTIFIED ORANGE JUICE
MAKES APPROX. 1 QUART

———

INGREDIENTS

Fresh Orange Juice: 1 quart
Olive Oil: 3 tbsp
Herbes de Provence: 1 ¾ cups

METHOD

Mix all the ingredients together
& leave to rest for 60 minutes.
Fine strain & bottle.
Keeps refrigerated for 1 week

SPICED APRICOT
CEYLON SHRUB
MAKES APPROX. 1 QUART

———

INGREDIENTS

Green Cardamom Pods: 5
Ceylon Tea: 1 ¼ cups (3 tea bags
brewed for 10 minutes, then strained)
Dried Apricots: about 1 cup
Superfine Sugar: 3 cups
Black Pepper: 1 ½ tsp
Salt: ½ tsp
Sherry Vinegar: 5 oz

METHOD

Place the cardamom pods in a pan
& dry fry over medium heat until toasted
& tinged brown. Transfer to a large
saucepan & add the tea, apricots, sugar,
pepper & salt & bring to a boil. Remove
from the heat & leave
to cool. Add the vinegar & stir.
Strain & bottle.
Keeps refrigerated for 1 month

CELERY ROOT TINCTURE
MAKES APPROX. 1 ⅔ CUPS

———

INGREDIENTS

Dehydrated Celery Root Peel
Dried Angelica: ½ tsp
Vegetable Glycerine (*see page 187*)

METHOD

Fill a 1-pint Kilner jar ⅔ full with celery
root peel. Add the angelica.
Top up with vegetable glycerine.
Rest in 3 cups water with a circulator
(*see page 184*) for at least 24 hours.
Cool & fine strain into a bottle.
Keeps for 6 months

CELERY ROOT SYRUP
MAKES 2 CUPS

———

INGREDIENTS

Water: 2 cups
Sugar: 2 cups
Celery Root Scraps: 9 oz

METHOD

Add all the ingredients to a saucepan
over medium heat & bring to a boil.
Reduce the heat, cover with a
lid & simmer for 30 minutes.
Cool & strain into bottles.
Keeps for 1 month

CLOUDBERRY CORDIAL
MAKES APPROX. 3 ¼ CUPS

—

INGREDIENTS
Honey: 2 cups
Hot Water: 2 cups
Cloudberries: 9 oz

METHOD
Add the honey to the water in a
large bowl & stir to dissolve. Add
the cloudberries & press them gently
to squeeze out the color. Leave
for 24 hours. Strain & bottle.
(The cloudberries can be eaten
over vanilla ice cream!)
Keeps for 3 months

PINE TREE SYRUP
MAKES APPROX. 3 ¼ CUPS

—

INGREDIENTS
Pine Tree Needles: 1 lb
Superfine Sugar: 2 ½ cups
Water: 2 cups

METHOD
Add the pine needles to the sugar
& water in a bowl & stir until the sugar
has dissolved. Vacuum pack & sous vide
(*see page 186*) for 60 minutes at 194°F.
Leave to cool. Strain & bottle.
Keeps refrigerated for 1 month

PINEAPPLE TEPACHE
MAKES APPROX. 1 QUART

—

INGREDIENTS
Pineapple: 1
Sugar: about ½ cup
Filtered Water: 1 quart

METHOD
Peel, core & chop the pineapple & add to
a Mason jar with the sugar & water &
muddle. Leave for 4 days at room
temperature. Fine strain & bottle.
Keeps refrigerated for 2 weeks

SPICED PEACH CORDIAL
MAKES APPROX. 3 ¼ CUPS

—

INGREDIENTS
Fresh Root Ginger: 1-inch piece
Freshly Pressed Peach Juice: 2 cups
Granulated White Sugar: 2 ½ cups
Cinnamon Sticks: 4
Ground Black Peppercorns: 1 tsp
Salt: Little Pinch

METHOD
Fill a basin with water & place an
immersion circulator (*see page 184*) inside set
at 135°F. Peel & thinly slice the ginger & add
to a Mason jar with all the other ingredients.
Seal the jar & place in the water. Leave for 2
hours. Carefully remove & transfer to an ice
bath until room temperature. Strain
through chinois & check for any floating
particles. Strain again through a 400 micron
super bag (*see page 186*), if needed & bottle.
Keeps refrigerated for 1 month

PROFILE

Herbal & Floral

PLANTS

Peas
Hay
Rosemary
Thyme
Spearmint
Hops

FREE FROM

Sugar
Sweeteners
Common Allergens

SEEDLIP

GARDEN 108

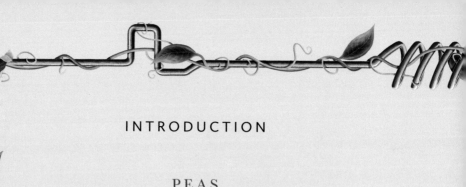

INTRODUCTION

PEAS
Pisum sativum

A delicacy in the 17th century, platters of freshly picked peas were offered by kings to wow their guests at banquets. Peas are nitrogen fixing (good for the soil) & there is more protein in a cup of peas than in an egg, more fiber than in a slice of whole-grain bread & more vitamin C than in 2 apples. They bring all those fresh green notes to Seedlip Garden 108. Eat your peas, please.

HAY
Lolium multiflorum

Hay is typically a blend of grasses, such as ryegrass, timothy & brome with alfalfa & clover. Its green & dry flavors (baking vegetables in hay is a must!) are unique to the specific blend we use – an excellent ryegrass hay grown on our farm each year.

ROSEMARY
Rosmarinus officinalis

A woody, perennial herb with fragrant leaves native to the Mediterranean region, rosemary brings a really herbaceous character to the Garden 108 blend. The name derives from the Latin for dew (*ros*) & sea (*marinus*) – "Dew of the Sea."

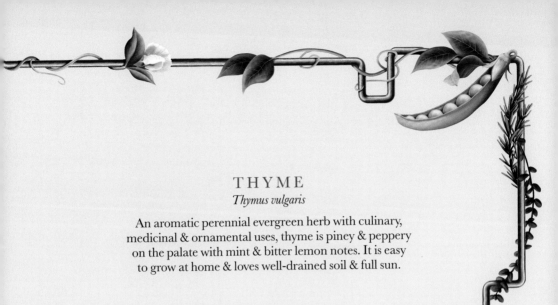

THYME
Thymus vulgaris

An aromatic perennial evergreen herb with culinary,
medicinal & ornamental uses, thyme is piney & peppery
on the palate with mint & bitter lemon notes. It is easy
to grow at home & loves well-drained soil & full sun.

SPEARMINT
Mentha spicata

The name derives from its pointed leaf tips & this
perennial herb is almost too easy to grow at home – it has
a habit of taking over! Spearmint brings the bright,
menthol freshness to the top notes of Garden 108.

HOPS
Humulus lupulus

The first documented cultivation of hops was in AD 736
in Germany & in 1524 the first British hops were grown.
Most commonly used in beer, hops bring slightly bitter
green & peppery notes to our blend.

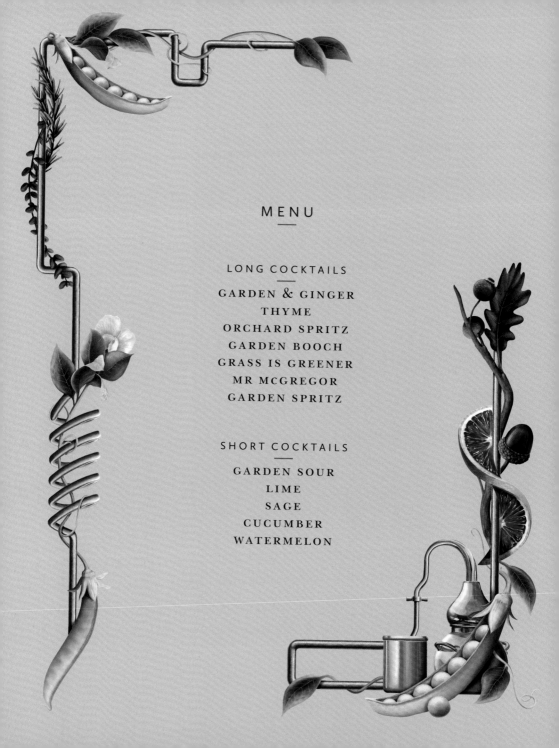

MENU

LONG COCKTAILS

GARDEN & GINGER
THYME
ORCHARD SPRITZ
GARDEN BOOCH
GRASS IS GREENER
MR McGREGOR
GARDEN SPRITZ

SHORT COCKTAILS

GARDEN SOUR
LIME
SAGE
CUCUMBER
WATERMELON

GARDEN 108
LONG COCKTAILS · SHORT COCKTAILS

CHAPTER
3

GARDEN & GINGER

GARDEN 108 · GINGER ALE · ROSEMARY

—

In herbal folklore, rosemary symbolizes remembrance and fidelity & is often included in wedding ceremonies.

INGREDIENTS

—

Garden 108: 2 oz
Fever-Tree Ginger Ale: Top
Ice: Cubed
Garnish: Rosemary Sprig
Glass: Tall

METHOD

—

Fill a tall glass with ice

Add Garden 108

Top with ginger ale

Garnish with a sprig of rosemary

THYME

GARDEN 108 · HERBS · TONIC · LEMON THYME

—

In the 18th century thyme was recommended as a hangover cure.

INGREDIENTS
—

Garden 108: 2 oz
Fever-Tree Mediterrean Tonic: Top
Ice: Cubed
Garnish: Lemon Thyme Sprig
Glass: Tall

METHOD
—

Fill a tall glass with ice

Add Garden 108

Top with tonic

Garnish with a sprig of lemon thyme

ORCHARD SPRITZ

GARDEN 108 · APPLE · PEAR · BUBBLES

—

Granny Smith apples were named after Maria Ann Smith,
who first cultivated them in Australia in 1868.

INGREDIENTS

—

Garden 108: 2 oz
Quality Nonalcoholic Sparkling Wine: 1 tbsp
Orchard Cordial (*see page 118*): 1 tbsp
Soda: Top
Ice: Cubed
Garnish: Apple Blossom or 3 Slices of Green Apple
Glass: Wine

METHOD

—

Fill a wineglass with ice

Add the Garden 108, sparkling wine
& Orchard Cordial & stir gently

Top with soda

Garnish with apple blossom
or 3 slices of green apple

GARDEN BOOCH

GARDEN 108 · KOMBUCHA · MINT

—

Mint derives its name from the ancient Greek
mythical character Minthe, a river nymph.

INGREDIENTS

—

Garden 108: 2 oz
Lemongrass Kombucha (*see page 185*): Top
Ice: Cubed
Garnish: Mint Leaf
Glass: Tumbler

METHOD

—

Fill a tumbler with ice

Add Garden 108

Top with Lemongrass Kombucha

Garnish with a mint leaf

GRASS IS GREENER

GARDEN 108 · MEADOW · GRASS · CUCUMBER FLOWER

—

*Wimbledon's grass tennis courts are thought
to be the most expensive lawns in the world.*

INGREDIENTS
—

Garden 108: 2 oz
Meadow Syrup (*see page 118*): ¾ oz
Cut Grass Glyncture (*see page 118*): 3 drops
Soda: Top
Ice: Hand-Cut Block
Garnish: Cucumber Flower
Glass: Tumbler

METHOD
—

Add the Garden 108, Meadow Syrup &
Cut Grass Glyncture to a tumbler over ice

Top with soda

Garnish with a cucumber flower

MR MCGREGOR

GARDEN 108 · SUGAR SNAP · CUCUMBER · CARROT

———

Until the 17th century, the only edible carrots were black, white, red & purple. Orange carrots were created by selective breeding in the Netherlands as a tribute to the ruling House of Orange.

INGREDIENTS
———

Garden 108: 2 oz
Sugar Snap Shrub (*see page 118*): ¾ oz
Cucumber Soda: Top
Ice: Cubed
Garnish: Carrot Slice
Glass: Tall

METHOD
———

Fill a tall glass with ice

Add the Garden 108 & Sugar Snap Shrub

Top with cucumber soda

Garnish with a carrot slice

GARDEN SPRITZ

GARDEN 108 · VERJUS · ELDERFLOWER · CELERY

—

Elderflowers have 5 petals.

INGREDIENTS
—

Garden 108: 2 oz
Verjus (White Grape Juice): 1 tbsp
Elderflower Cordial: 1 tbsp
Celery Droplets (*see page 184*): 3 drops
Soda: Top
Ice: Cubed
Garnish: Borage Flowers & Pea Tendrils
Glass: Wine

METHOD
—

Add ice to a wineglass

Add the Garden 108, verjus, elderflower
cordial & Celery Droplets

Top with soda

Garnish with borage flowers & pea tendrils

GARDEN SOUR

GARDEN 108 · APPLE · LEMON · ROSEMARY · THYME

—

The number 108 refers to the average number of days
it takes to sow, grow & hand-harvest our peas.

INGREDIENTS

—

Garden 108: 2 oz
Cloudy Apple Juice: 1 oz
Fresh Lemon Juice: 1 tbsp
Cider Vinegar: 1 tsp
Rosemary Sprig: 1
Thyme Sprig: 1
Sugar Syrup (*see page 186*): 2 tsp
Egg White: 1
Ice: Cubed
Garnish: Rosemary Sprig
Glass: Coupe

METHOD

—

Add all the ingredients to a shaker with ice & shake

Double strain into a coupe glass

Garnish with a sprig of rosemary

LIME

—

Limes are 88% water, 10% carbohydrates
& less than 1% each of fat & protein.

INGREDIENTS
—

Garden 108: 2 oz
Sugar Syrup (*see page 186*): 1 oz
Fresh Lime Juice: 2 tsp
Ice: Cubed
Garnish: Cucumber Ribbon
Glass: Coupe

METHOD
—

Add all the ingredients to a shaker with ice & shake

Strain into a coupe glass

Garnish with a cucumber ribbon

SAGE

—

There are more than 900 species of sage around the world.

INGREDIENTS

—

Garden 108: 2 oz
Endothermic Verjus (*see page 119*): 1 tbsp
Nettle & Pear Shrub (*see page 119*): 2 tsp
Sage Glyncture (*see page 119*): 3 drops
Ice: Cubed
Garnish: Nasturtium Leaf
Glass: Coupe

METHOD

—

Add a scoop of ice to a mixing glass

Add all the other ingredients & stir for 30 seconds

Strain into a coupe glass

Garnish with a nasturtium leaf

CUCUMBER

GARDEN 108 · CUCUMBER · LEMON THYME

—

There can be a 68°F difference between the inside of a cucumber & the actual temperature outside (hence the phrase "as cool as a cucumber").

INGREDIENTS
—
Garden 108: 2 oz
Cucumber & Lemon Shrub (*see page 119*): ¾ oz
Salt: Pinch
Ice: Cubed
Garnish: Lemon Thyme Sprig
Glass: Coupe

METHOD
—
Add all the ingredients to a mixing glass with ice & stir

Strain into a coupe glass

Garnish with a sprig of lemon thyme

Gardener's Latin   BILL NEAL   HALE

WATERMELON

—

Japanese farmers have been growing cube-shaped
watermelons for more than 40 years!

INGREDIENTS
—

Garden 108: 2 oz
Watermelon & Basil Shrub (*see page 120*): 1 oz
Egg White/Aquafaba (*see page 184*): 1 tbsp
Ice: Cubed
Garnish: Basil Leaf
Glass: Coupe

METHOD
—

Add all the ingredients except the ice to a shaker & dry shake

Add the ice & shake again

Double strain into a coupe glass

Garnish with a basil leaf

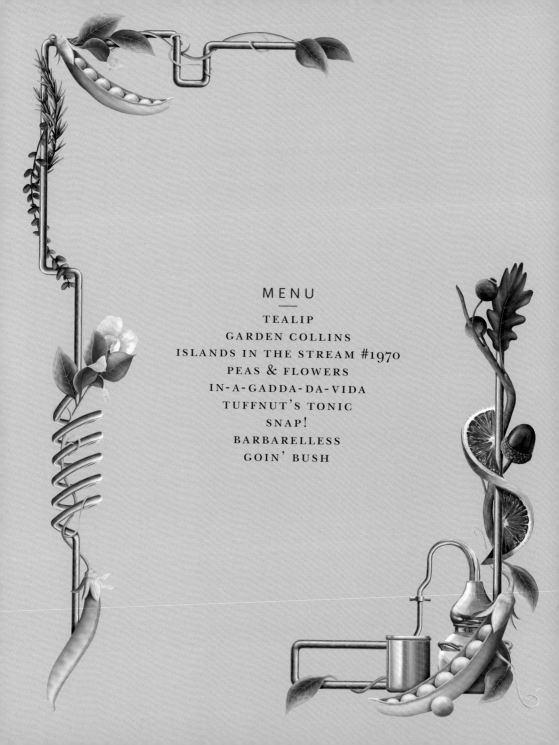

MENU

—

TEALIP

GARDEN COLLINS

ISLANDS IN THE STREAM #1970

PEAS & FLOWERS

IN-A-GADDA-DA-VIDA

TUFFNUT'S TONIC

SNAP!

BARBARELLESS

GOIN' BUSH

GARDEN 108

GUEST COCKTAILS

A selection of cocktails from some of the world's best bartenders

CHAPTER
4

TEALIP

—

XAV LANDAIS – SEXY FISH, LONDON

Bar with the largest Japanese whisky collection in Europe

INGREDIENTS
—

Garden 108: 1 oz
Bergamot Purée: 1 oz
G&Tea Cordial (*see page 120*): 1 oz
Ice: Hand-Cut Block
Garnish: None
Glass: Teacup

METHOD
—

Add all the ingredients to a mixing glass & shake

Fine strain into a teacup over an ice block

GARDEN COLLINS

GARDEN 108 · APPLE · ELDERFLOWER · CUCUMBER · BASIL

—

JACK MCGARRY – THE DEAD RABBIT & BLACKTAIL, NEW YORK CITY

5th & 32nd Best Bars in the World – World's 50 Best Bar Awards 2017

INGREDIENTS

—

Garden 108: 2 oz
Fresh Lemon Juice: 1 tbsp
Freshly Pressed Granny Smith Apple Juice: 1 tbsp
Elderflower Lemon Sherbet (*see page 120*): 1 oz
Cucumber Soda: Top
Ice: Cubed
Garnish: Basil Leaf
Glass: Tall

METHOD

—

Add the Garden 108, lemon juice,
apple juice & Elderflower Lemon Sherbet
to a shaker with ice & shake

Strain into a tall glass over ice

Top with cucumber soda

Garnish with a basil leaf

ISLANDS IN THE STREAM #1970

GARDEN 108 · PINK GRAPEFRUIT · MANGOSTEEN

—

AGUNG PRABOWO – THE OLD MAN BAR, HONG KONG

5th Best Bar in Asia – Asia's 50 Best Bar Awards 2018

INGREDIENTS

(4 SERVINGS)

—

Garden 108: 1 ½ cups
Clarified Pink Grapefruit Juice (*see page 121*): 2 ½ cups
Clear Mangosteen Juice (*see page 121*): ¼ cup
Water: ⅓ cup
Sugar Syrup (*see page 186*): 6 tbsp
Salt: 2 pinches
Ice: Cubed
Garnish: Grapefruit Zest & Mangosteen Wheel
Glass: Tall

METHOD

—

Add all the ingredients to a Twist & Sparkle bottle
(these are used by bartenders to carbonate drinks)

Pour into 4 tall glasses over ice

Garnish with grapefruit zest & a mangosteen wheel

PEAS & FLOWERS

GARDEN 108 · HONEY · LEMON BALM · PEA TENDRILS

—

LUKE WHEARTY – OPERATION DAGGER, SINGAPORE

24ᵗʰ Best Bar in the World – World's 50 Best Bar Awards 2017

INGREDIENTS

—

Garden 108: 2 oz
Honey Syrup (*see page 185*): ¾ oz
Lemon Balm Vinegar (*see page 121*): 1 tbsp
Soda: Top
Ice: Cubed
Garnish: Pea Tendrils & Seasonal Edible Flowers (if available)
Glass: Tall

METHOD

—

Fill a tall glass with ice

Add the Garden 108, honey syrup & Lemon Balm Vinegar

Top with soda

Garnish with pea tendrils & seasonal edible flowers

IN-A-GADDA-DA-VIDA

GARDEN 108 · PUFF PASTRY · PEAR · THAI LIME LEAF

—

CHRIS HYSTED-ADAMS – BLACK PEARL, MELBOURNE

22nd Best Bar in the World – World's 50 Best Bar Awards 2017

INGREDIENTS

—

Garden 108: 1 oz
Fresh Lime Juice: ¾ oz
Pear & Thai Lime Leaf Syrup (*see page 121*): ¾ oz
Puff Pastry Cream (*see page 122*): 1 oz
Egg White: 1
Mineral Water: 2 oz
Ice: Crushed
Garnish: Thai Lime Leaf Disc
Glass: Chilled Tall

METHOD

—

Spindle mix (*see page 186*) the Garden 108,
lime juice, Pear & Thai Lime Leaf Syrup,
Puff Pastry Cream & egg white in a mixing
glass with a small handful of crushed ice

When the ice has dissolved, pour the
mineral water into a chilled tall glass

Top with the mixed ingredients

Garnish with a lime leaf disc

TUFFNUT'S TONIC

GARDEN 108 · CUCUMBER · SHISO · DRAGON EYE

—

JIM MEEHAN – PDT, NEW YORK & HONG KONG
World Top 100 Bar – World's Best Bar Awards 2017

INGREDIENTS
—

Garden 108: 2 oz
Cucumber Wheels: 2
Shiso Leaf (*see page 186*): 1
Dragon Fruit Syrup (*see page 123*): 2 tsp
Fresh Lime Juice: 1 tbsp
East Imperial Tonic: 2 oz
Ice: Cubed
Garnish: Shiso Leaf
Glass: Tall

METHOD
—

Muddle the cucumber wheels & shiso leaf in a shaker
with the Dragon Fruit Syrup

Add the Garden 108 & lime juice & shake

Add the tonic then fine strain into a tall glass filled with ice

Garnish with a shiso leaf

SNAP!

GARDEN 108 · BUTTERMILK · SUGAR SNAP PEAS · TIMUT

—

ALEX KRATENA – EX BAR MANAGER OF ARTESIAN, LONDON
& CO-FOUNDER OF (P)OUR

INGREDIENTS
—

Garden 108: 1 ½ oz
Buttermilk Vinaigrette (*see page 123*): 1 ½ oz
Sugar Snap Pea Syrup (*see page 123*): 1 tbsp
Timut Pepper (*see page 187*): 1 pinch
Ice: Cubed
Garnish: 3 Timut Peppercorns
Glass: Chilled Coupe

METHOD
—

Add all the ingredients to a shaker with ice & shake

Strain into a chilled coupe glass

Garnish with 3 timut peppercorns

BARBARELLESS

GARDEN 108 · LIME · CHILE · RHUBARB

—

TESS POSTHUMUS – THE FLYING DUTCHMEN, AMSTERDAM

Top 10 International Bartender of the Year 2017, Tales of the Cocktail

INGREDIENTS
—

Garden 108: 1 ½ oz
Fresh Lime Juice: 1 tbsp
Grapefruit & Chile Syrup (*see page 123*): 1 tbsp
Salt: Pinch
Rhubarb Soda (*see page 186*): Top
Ice: Cubed
Garnish: Rhubarb Ribbon
Glass: Tall

METHOD
—

Add the Garden 108, lime juice, Grapefruit
& Chile Syrup & salt to a shaker & shake

Strain into a tall glass filled with ice

Top with rhubarb soda

Garnish with a rhubarb ribbon

GOIN' BUSH

GARDEN 108 · AVOCADO · EUCALYPTUS · GRAPE

—

IAIN GRIFFITHS – TRASH TIKI, SUPER LYAN & DANDELYAN

Dandelyan 2nd Best Bar in the World – World's 50 Best Bar Awards 2017

INGREDIENTS

—

Garden 108: 1 oz
Avocado Pit Honey (*see page 122*): 2 tsp
Fresh Grapefruit Juice: 1 tsp
Pea & Eucalyptus Soda (*see page 122*): Top
Ice: Cubed
Garnish: Compressed White Grape (*see page 122*)
Glass: Tall

METHOD

—

Add all the ingredients to a tall glass

Garnish with a compressed white grape

ORCHARD CORDIAL
MAKES APPROX. 2 ½ CUPS

—

INGREDIENTS
Superfine Sugar: 2 cups
Apple Juice: 1 cup
Pear Juice: 1 cup

METHOD
Add all the ingredients to a saucepan
& bring to a boil. Reduce the heat, cover
& simmer for 30 minutes. Leave to cool,
then strain into a bottle.
Keeps for 1 month

MEADOW SYRUP
MAKES APPROX. 1 ½ CUPS

—

INGREDIENTS
Meadowsweet: Handful
Sorrel: Handful
Honeysuckle: Handful
Water: 1 cup
Sugar: 1 ¼ cups
Malic Acid: 1 tsp

METHOD
Vacuum pack & sous vide (*see page 186*)
all the ingredients together for
60 minutes at 167°F.
Cool & strain into a bottle.
Keeps for 1 week

CUT GRASS GLYNCTURE
MAKES 1 ½ CUPS

—

INGREDIENTS
Freshly Cut & Washed Grass
Water: 3 oz
Vegetable Glycerine (*see page 187*): 1 cup

METHOD
Fill a 1-pint Mason jar ⅔ full with grass.
Add the water & vegetable glycerine
& seal. Refrigerate for 3 days.
Fine strain & bottle.
Keeps for 6 months

SUGAR SNAP
SHRUB
MAKES 1 CUP

—

INGREDIENTS
Sugar Snap Peas: 8 oz
Apple Cider Vinegar: 1 cup
Superfine Sugar: 1 ¼ cups

METHOD
Finely slice the peas & place in a
Mason jar with the other ingredients.
Muddle hard, then leave overnight.
Strain & bottle.
Keeps refrigerated for 2 weeks

ENDOTHERMIC VERJUS

MAKES 1 CUP

—

INGREDIENTS
Sansho Peppercorns: 15
Verjus (White Grape Juice): 1 cup

METHOD
Use a mortar & pestle to break open
the peppercorns. Add to a Mason jar
with the verjus & mix. Leave in the fridge
for 2 hours. Fine strain & bottle.
Keeps refrigerated for 2 weeks

SAGE GLYNCTURE

MAKES APPROX. 1 CUP

—

INGREDIENTS
Sage Leaves: 3 handfuls
Vegetable Glycerine (*see page 187*): ¾ cup
Water: ⅓ cup

METHOD
Fill a 1-pint Mason jar ⅔ full with
sage leaves. Cover with the vegetable
glycerine & water. Leave for 48 hours.
Fine strain & bottle.
Keeps for 6 months

NETTLE & PEAR SHRUB

MAKES 1 ⅔ CUPS

—

INGREDIENTS
Nettles: 3 ½ oz
Sliced Pears: 3
Apple Cider Vinegar: 1 cup
Superfine Sugar: 1 ¼ cups

METHOD
Add the nettles & pears to a
Mason jar & muddle. Add the vinegar
& sugar & stir. Leave for 24 hours.
Fine strain & bottle.
Keeps refrigerated for 1 month

CUCUMBER & LEMON SHRUB

MAKES 1 ⅔ CUPS

—

INGREDIENTS
Lemons: 3
Finely Sliced Cucumbers: 3
Apple Cider Vinegar: ¾ cup
Superfine Sugar: 1 cup

METHOD
Remove the peel from the lemons &
add to a Mason jar with the cucumbers
& muddle. Add the vinegar & sugar
& stir. Refrigerate for 24 hours.
Fine strain & bottle.
Keeps for 1 week

WATERMELON & BASIL SHRUB

MAKES 1 ⅔ CUPS

—

INGREDIENTS

Watermelon: ½
Basil: Handful
Apple Cider Vinegar: ¾ cup
Sugar: 1 cup

METHOD

Chop the watermelon flesh & add to a
Mason jar with the basil leaves & muddle.
Add the vinegar & sugar & shake. Leave
for 24 hours. Fine strain & bottle.
Keeps refrigerated for 1 month

BLUEBERRY SHRUB

MAKES APPROX. 3 ¼ CUPS

—

INGREDIENTS

Fresh Blueberries: 1 ¼ lb
Cider Vinegar: 1 ¼ cups
Superfine Sugar: 1 ½ cups
Garnish: Skewers of blueberries
(optional)

METHOD

Place the blueberries in a nonmetallic
container & add the vinegar. Cover
tightly & refrigerate for at least 3 days.
Pour through a sieve & press the berries
to release their juices. Pour the blueberry
liquid into a medium saucepan, add the
sugar & boil for 3 minutes, stirring
occasionally. Remove from the heat
& leave to cool. Bottle & chill.
Keeps refrigerated for 1 month

G&TEA CORDIAL

MAKES 1 ¼ QUARTS

—

INGREDIENTS

G&Tea flavored tea bags
(Fortnum & Mason): 6
Boiling Water: 3 ⅓ cups
Sugar: 4 cups

METHOD

Steep the tea bags in the water for
10 minutes. Strain & add the sugar.
Leave to cool.
Keeps for 1 month

ELDERFLOWER LEMON SHERBET

MAKES 1 QUART

—

INGREDIENTS

Lemons: 6
Sugar: 3 ¾ cups
Fresh Lemon Juice: 1 ½ cups
Elderflower Tea (cold infusion): 1 ½ cups

METHOD

Remove the zest from the lemons & add
to a bowl with the sugar. Mix thoroughly
so the oils from the zest begin to express
into the sugar. Leave at room temperature
for at least 1 hour (or vacuum pack
the zest & sugar for faster results – *see page
187*). Tip the mixture into a saucepan &
add the lemon juice & tea. Place over
medium heat & cook at 140°F, stirring
regularly, for 30 minutes, until the sugar
has completely dissolved. Pour through
a fine mesh strainer & bottle.
Keeps refrigerated for 1 month

CLARIFIED PINK GRAPEFRUIT JUICE
MAKES 1 LITER

—

INGREDIENTS

Grapefruit Juice: 1 liter (34 fl oz)
Pectinex Ultra SP-L (*see page 186*): 2g
Chitosan (*see page 184*): 2g
Kieselsol (*see page 183*): 2g

METHOD

Add the ingredients to a centrifuge
(*see page 184*) & spin for 5 minutes
at high speed. Place the clarified juice
into a separate container.
Keeps refrigerated for 1 week

CLEAR MANGOSTEEN JUICE
MAKES 1 QUART

—

INGREDIENTS

Mangosteen: 3 ⅓ lb
Superfine Sugar: 2 ½ cups
Water: 2 cups
Pectinex Ultra SP-L (*see page 186*): 1 tsp

METHOD

Remove the mangosteen pulp & place
in a blender with the other ingredients
in a heavy-duty blender. Blend until the
sugar has dissolved. Place half the
mixture in a centrifuge (*see page 184*)
& spin at the highest speed (4000 rpm)
for 25 minutes. Strain through a
cheesecloth into a bottle. Repeat with
the second half of the mixture.
Keeps refrigerated for 1 week

LEMON BALM VINEGAR
MAKES 1 QUART

—

INGREDIENTS

Lemon Pelargonium Leaves
(*see page 185*): 1 ¾ oz
Apple Cider Vinegar: 1 quart

METHOD

Add both the ingredients to a saucepan
& bring to a boil. Boil for 3 minutes.
Remove from the heat & leave to cool.
Strain & bottle.
Keeps refrigerated for 1 month

PEAR & THAI LIME LEAF SYRUP
MAKES APPROX. 1 CUP

—

INGREDIENTS

Nashi Pears: 3
Superfine Sugar: about 1 ¼ cups
Large Thai Lime Leaves: 2

METHOD

Juice the pears & measure the liquid.
Pour into a saucepan & add the same
weight of sugar. Add the Thai lime
leaves & heat very gently, stirring until
the sugar has dissolved. Remove from the
heat & steep for 1 hour. Strain & bottle.
Keeps for 1 month

PUFF PASTRY CREAM

MAKES 2 CUPS

—

INGREDIENTS

Puff Pastry Sheets: 2
Heavy Cream: 2 cups

METHOD

Preheat the oven to 325°F.
Place the sheets of puff pastry between
2 baking sheets. Bake until golden brown
& crisp. Break into smaller pieces &
submerge in the cream in a nonreactive
bowl. Cover with plastic wrap &
refrigerate overnight. Strain, making
sure to squeeze all the infused cream
from any lumps of pastry. Bottle.
Keeps refrigerated for 1 week

AVOCADO PIT HONEY

MAKES 1 QUART

—

INGREDIENTS

Avocado Pits: 6
Local Honey: 4 cups
Boiling Water: 1 cup

METHOD

Clean & dry the avocado pits.
Finely grate them, then place in a dry
pan. Toast over medium heat until
pinkish-red. Remove from the heat & tip
into a bowl with the honey & boiling
water. Leave to rest for 1 day.
Strain & store in jars.
Keeps for 6 months

PEA & EUCALYPTUS SODA

MAKES APPROX. 3 ¼ CUPS

—

INGREDIENTS

Freeze-Dried Peas: ½ tsp
Dried Eucalyptus: Pinch
Boiling Water: 3 ¼ cups
Malic Acid: Pinch
Superfine Sugar: 1 tsp

METHOD

Blend the peas & eucalyptus in a spice
grinder. Add to a bowl with the boiling
water, the malic acid & the sugar. Brew for
5 minutes, stirring constantly. Strain into
bottles. Leave to cool, then chill. Use an ISI
Soda Syphon with 1 Co2 & 1 No2 bulbs.
Keeps for 1 week

COMPRESSED WHITE GRAPES

MAKES 8 OZ

—

INGREDIENTS

Underripe White Grapes: 8 oz
Dried Avocado Leaf: ⅓ oz
Boiling Water: 2 cups
Superfine Sugar: ¼ cup
White Wine Vinegar: 2 tsp

METHOD

Stem the grapes & pierce them a few
times with a toothpick. Brew the avocado
leaf in the boiling water for 10 minutes.
Strain & leave to cool. Add the sugar &
vinegar to the brew & stir to dissolve the
sugar. Place in a Kilner jar with the
grapes & seal. Refrigerate for 3 days.
Keeps for 1 week

DRAGON FRUIT SYRUP
MAKES APPROX. 2 CUPS

—

INGREDIENTS
Dried Dragon Eye (Logan): 1 ¾ oz
Sugar Syrup (*see page 186*): 2 ⅓ cups

METHOD
Measure the ingredients into a saucepan
& place over medium heat.
Simmer gently for 5 minutes.
Remove from the heat & fine strain.
Leave to cool, then bottle.
Keeps refrigerated for 1 month

BUTTERMILK VINAIGRETTE
MAKES APPROX. 2 CUPS

—

INGREDIENTS
Organic Buttermilk: 2 cups
White Balsamic Vinegar: 3 ½ tbsp
Extra Virgin Olive Oil: ½ tsp
Salt: Pinch

METHOD
Using an immersion blender, blend
all ingredients until fully emulsified.
Store in an airtight container.
Keeps refrigerated for 3 days

SUGAR SNAP PEA SYRUP
MAKES 3 ½ CUPS

—

INGREDIENTS
Sugar Snap Peas: 8 oz
Rich Sugar Syrup (*see page 186*): 2 ½ cups

METHOD
Roughly chop the peas & place in a
non-reactive container with the syrup.
Infuse for 24 hours. Strain & place
in an airtight container.
Keeps refrigerated for 2 weeks

GRAPEFRUIT &
CHILE SYRUP
MAKES APPROX. 2 CUPS

—

INGREDIENTS
Red Grapefruits: 3
Superfine Sugar: 1 ¼ cups
Water: 1 cup
Sliced Red Chile: 1

METHOD
Grate the peel of the grapefruits into
a bowl. Add the sugar & stir vigorously.
Crush the peels into the sugar until
slushy. Cover & leave overnight.
Place the water in a saucepan & bring
to a boil. Stir in the citrus sugar & add
the sliced chile. Simmer for 3 minutes
to dissolve the sugar. Remove from
the heat & leave to cool. Strain the
liquid, discarding the peel,
chile & seeds. Bottle.
Keeps for 1 month

PROFILE

Citrus & Warm

PLANTS

Plants
Bitter Orange
Blood Orange
Mandarin
Ginger
Lemongrass
Lemon

FREE FROM

Sugar
Sweeteners
Common Allergens

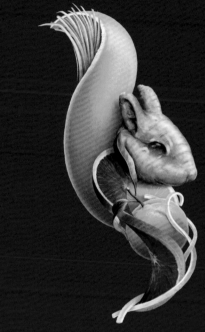

SEEDLIP

—

GROVE 42

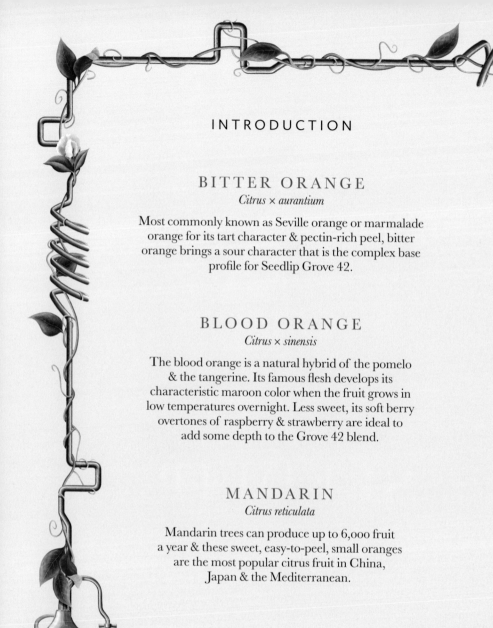

INTRODUCTION

BITTER ORANGE

Citrus × aurantium

Most commonly known as Seville orange or marmalade
orange for its tart character & pectin-rich peel, bitter
orange brings a sour character that is the complex base
profile for Seedlip Grove 42.

BLOOD ORANGE

Citrus × sinensis

The blood orange is a natural hybrid of the pomelo
& the tangerine. Its famous flesh develops its
characteristic maroon color when the fruit grows in
low temperatures overnight. Less sweet, its soft berry
overtones of raspberry & strawberry are ideal to
add some depth to the Grove 42 blend.

MANDARIN

Citrus reticulata

Mandarin trees can produce up to 6,000 fruit
a year & these sweet, easy-to-peel, small oranges
are the most popular citrus fruit in China,
Japan & the Mediterranean.

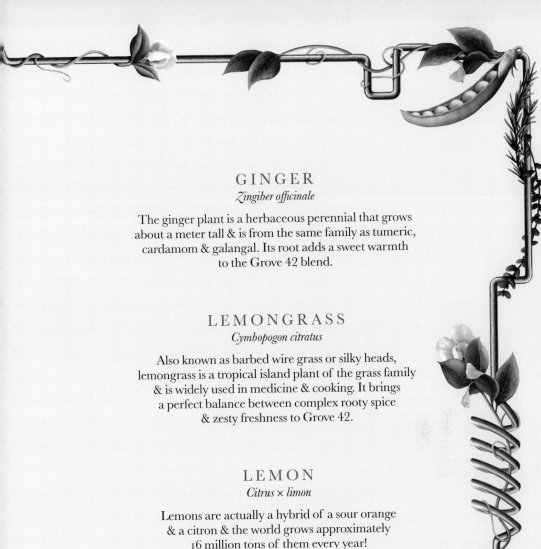

GINGER
Zingiber officinale

The ginger plant is a herbaceous perennial that grows
about a meter tall & is from the same family as tumeric,
cardamom & galangal. Its root adds a sweet warmth
to the Grove 42 blend.

LEMONGRASS
Cymbopogon citratus

Also known as barbed wire grass or silky heads,
lemongrass is a tropical island plant of the grass family
& is widely used in medicine & cooking. It brings
a perfect balance between complex rooty spice
& zesty freshness to Grove 42.

LEMON
Citrus × limon

Lemons are actually a hybrid of a sour orange
& a citron & the world grows approximately
16 million tons of them every year!

MENU

LONG COCKTAILS

GROVE & GINGER
PEEL
MALT
THOROUGHBRED
WOOD
CLEMENTS
CASCARA
CITRUS

SHORT COCKTAILS

MANGO
BLOSSOM
MILK PUNCH
HONEY
CASHEW PUNCH

GROVE 42
LONG COCKTAILS · SHORT COCKTAILS

CHAPTER
5

GROVE & GINGER

GROVE 42 · GINGER ALE · LEMON

—

The Number 42 refers to 1542, the year the word orange
was first used to describe a color.

INGREDIENTS
—

Grove 42: 2 oz
Fever-Tree Ginger Ale: Top
Ice: Cubed
Garnish: Lemon Slice
Glass: Tall

METHOD
—

Fill a tall glass with ice

Add Grove 42

Top with ginger ale

Garnish with a lemon slice

PEEL

—

There are 1.3 billion tons of food wasted every year.
Here's the perfect use for those unwanted carrot peelings.

INGREDIENTS

—

Grove 42: 2 oz
Carrot Cordial (*see page 166*): ¾ oz
Soda: Top
Ice: Cubed
Garnish: Sage Leaf
Glass: Tumbler

METHOD

—

Fill a tumbler with ice

Add the Grove 42 & Carrot Cordial

Top with soda

Garnish with a sage leaf

MALT

GROVE 42 · MALT · SMOKE · LEMON · ORANGE

—

*Roasted barley was used as a coffee substitute during
the First & Second World Wars in Italy.*

INGREDIENTS
—

Grove 42: 2 oz
Malt Syrup (*see page 166*): ¾ oz
Bonfire Glyncture (*see page 166*): 2 drops
Fresh Lemon Juice: 2 tsp
Soda: Top
Ice: Cubed
Garnish: Orange Slice
Glass: Tall

METHOD
—

Fill a tall glass with ice

Add the Grove 42, Malt Syrup, Bonfire Glyncture & lemon juice

Top with soda

Garnish with an orange slice

THOROUGHBRED

GROVE 42 · GINGER · LIME

—

A male mule is called a john.

INGREDIENTS
—

Grove 42: 2 oz
Ginger Beer: Top
Ice: Cubed
Garnish: Lime Wheel
Glass: Tumbler

METHOD
—

Fill a tumbler with ice

Add the Grove 42

Top with ginger beer

Garnish with a lime wheel

WOOD

GROVE 42 · CHAR · BLOOD ORANGE

—

The blood orange was once reserved for royalty & the very privileged,
so it features in many early European paintings, mosaics & poems.

INGREDIENTS
—

Grove 42: 2 oz
Fever-Tree Smoked Ginger Ale: Top
Ice: Cubed
Garnish: Blood Orange Wheel
Glass: Tumbler

METHOD
—

Fill a tumbler with ice

Add the Grove 42

Top with the ginger ale

Garnish with a wheel of blood orange

CLEMENTS

GROVE 42 · SUNSHINE · FLOWERS

—

One million Earths could fit inside the Sun.

INGREDIENTS
—

Grove 42: 2 oz
Sunshine Syrup (*see page 166*) ¾ oz
Soda: Top
Ice: Cubed
Garnish: Seasonal Flower
Glass: Champagne Flute

METHOD
—

Add the Grove 42, Sunshine Syrup & ice to a shaker & shake

Strain into a Champagne flute

Top with soda

Garnish with a flower

CASCARA

—

Cascaras are the dried skins of coffee cherries.

INGREDIENTS

—

Grove 42: 2 oz
Cascara Syrup (*see page 167*): 1 tbsp
Soda: Top
Ice: Cubed
Garnish: Hibiscus Flowers
Glass: Tumbler

METHOD

—

Fill a tumbler with ice

Add the Grove 42 & Cascara Syrup

Top with soda

Garnish with hibiscus flowers

CITRUS

GROVE 42 · BUBBLES · CITRUS

—

Joseph Priestly invented carbonated water in 1767.

INGREDIENTS

—

Grove 42: 2 oz
Sugar-free Lemon & Lime Soda: Top
Ice: Cubed
Garnish: Blood Orange Slice
Glass: Tall

METHOD

—

Fill a tall glass with ice

Add Grove 42

Top with soda

Garnish with a blood orange slice

MANGO

GROVE 42 · YUZU · MANGO

—

*More fresh mangoes are eaten around the world
each day than any other fruit*

INGREDIENTS

—

Grove 42: 2 oz
Yuzu Verjus (*see page 167*): ¾ oz
Mango Drops (*see page 167*): 3
Ice: Cubed
Garnish (optional): Orange Twist
Glass: Coupe

METHOD

—

Add all the ingredients to a mixing glass
filled with ice & stir for 30 seconds

Strain into a coupe glass

Garnish with an orange twist (optional)

BLOSSOM

GROVE 42 · VERTICAL CITRUS

—

June 27th is National Orange Blossom Day in the USA.

INGREDIENTS

(14 SERVINGS)

—

Grove 42: 2 oz
Fresh Orange Juice: 1 oz
Fresh Lemon Juice: 2 tsp
Cider Vinegar: 1 tsp
Lemongrass Stalk: 1
Sugar Syrup (*see page 186*): 1 tbsp
Orange Blossom Water (*see page 185*): 1 drop
Egg White: 1
Ice: Cubed
Garnish: Orange Leaf
Glass: Coupe

METHOD

—

Add all the ingredients to a shaker with the ice & hard shake

Double strain into a coupe glass

Garnish with an orange leaf

MILK PUNCH

GROVE 42 · ALMOND · CITRUS

—

*Milk punch was first recorded in William Sacheverell's 1688 travelogue
of the Scottish isle of Iona. This is the first nonalcoholic version!*

INGREDIENTS

(14 SERVINGS)

—

Grove 42: 3 cups
Almond Milk: ½ cup
Whole Milk: ½ cup
Rooibos & Turmeric Cordial (*see page 167*): ¾ cup
Fresh Lemon Juice: ¼ cup
Fresh Grapefruit Juice: ¼ cup
Ice: Hand-Cut Block
Garnish: Blood Orange Peel
Glass: Tumbler

METHOD

—

Bring the almond & whole milk to a simmer over medium heat

Pour into a large pitcher

Mix the Grove 42, cordial & juices in a separate jug

Slowly add this to the milk & allow it to curdle

Leave for 30 minutes, then strain through a coffee filter

Bottle & store for up to 1 week

Serve with ice & garnish with a blood orange twist

HONEY

—

While excavating Egyptian tombs, archaeologists found 3,000-year-old honey that was still perfectly edible.

INGREDIENTS

—

Grove 42: 2 oz
Gorse & Beeswax Shrub (*see page 168*): ¾ oz
Fresh Mandarin Juice: ¾ oz
Honey Droplet: 1
Ice: Cubed
Garnish: Honey Drip
Glass: Tumbler

METHOD

—

Add the ingredients to a shaker
without ice & throw several times

Add ice & shake

Double strain into a tumbler

Garnish with a drip of honey

CASHEW PUNCH

GROVE 42 · CASHEW · GINGER

—

Raw cashews are green & cashews are actually a seed & not a nut.

INGREDIENTS

(14 SERVINGS)

—

Grove 42: 3 cups
Cashew Milk: ½ cup
Whole Milk: ½ cup
Ginger Cordial: 6 tbsp
Fresh Lemon Juice: ⅔ cup
Ice: Cubed
Garnish: Candied Ginger Cube with Sugar Coating Removed
Glass: Coupe

METHOD

—

Bring the cashew & whole milk to a simmer over medium heat

Pour into a large pitcher

Mix the Grove 42, cordial & juice in a separate jug

Slowly add this to the milk & allow it to curdle

Leave for 30 minutes, then strain through a coffee filter

Bottle & store for up to 1 week

Add ice & strain into a coupe glass

Garnish with de-sugared candied ginger cube

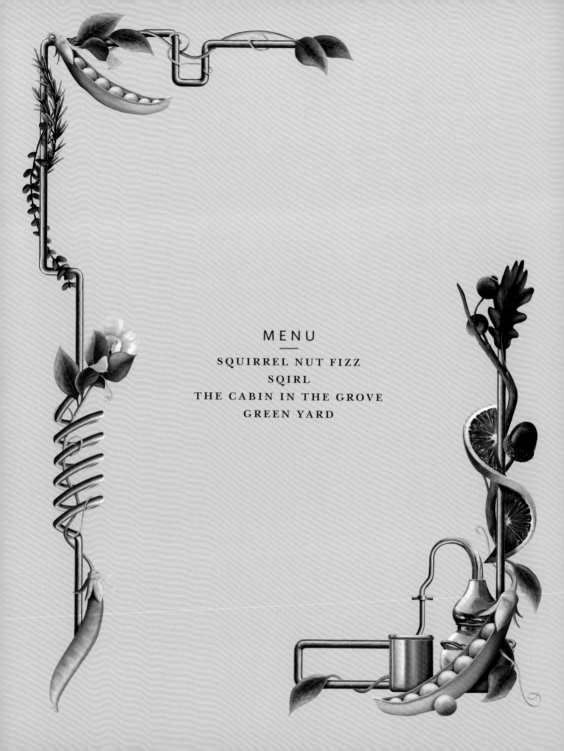

MENU

—

SQUIRREL NUT FIZZ
SQIRL
THE CABIN IN THE GROVE
GREEN YARD

GROVE 42

GUEST COCKTAILS

A selection of cocktails from some of the world's best bartenders

CHAPTER

6

SQUIRREL NUT FIZZ

GROVE 42 · RIBENA · VANILLA · PEANUT

—

RYAN CHETIYAWARDANA – CUB, SUPER LYAN, DANDELYAN, LONDON
Dandelyan 2nd Best Bar in the World – World's 50 Best Bar Awards 2017

INGREDIENTS
—

Grove 42: 2 oz
Ribena Blackcurrant Soda: 1 tsp
Honey Syrup (*see page 185*): 2 tsp
Fresh Blood Orange Juice: 1 tbsp
Fresh Lemon Juice: 1 tbsp
Egg White: 1
Vanilla Peanut Milk (*see page 187*): 1 tsp
Chilled Soda: Top
Ice: Cubed
Garnish: Rosemary Dust (*see page 168*)
Glass: Chilled Tall

METHOD
—

Add all the ingredients except the soda
to a shaker without ice & dry shake

Add ice & shake again

Double strain into a chilled tall glass

Top with chilled soda

Garnish with rosemary dust

SQIRL

GROVE 42 · YUZU · CARDAMOM

—

MATT WHILEY – SCOUT, LONDON
World Top 100 Bar – World's Best Bar Awards 2017

INGREDIENTS
—

Grove 42: 2 oz
Yuzu Juice (*see page 187*): ¾ oz
Cardamom Syrup (*see page 168*): 1 tbsp
Ice: Crushed
Glass: Continental Beer
Garnish: Mint Leaf & Orange Disc

METHOD
—

Add all the ingredients, including 1 small scoop crushed ice,
to a blender & blitz until smooth

Pour into a Continental beer glass & serve as a slushy

Garnish with a mint leaf & orange disc

THE CABIN
IN THE GROVE
GROVE 42 · PINE · PLUM · LAPSANG

—

ROB SIMPSON – THE CLOVE CLUB, LONDON
33rd Best Restaurant in the World – World's 50 Best Restaurant Awards 2018

INGREDIENTS
—
Grove 42: 2 oz
Pine-smoked Blood Orange Juice (*see page 169*): ¾ oz
Pine Cordial (*see page 169*): ¾ oz
Spiced Grilled Plum Purée (*see page 169*): 1 tbsp
Cold-Brewed Lapsang Souchong Tea: 1 tbsp
Salt: Pinch
Ice: Hand-Cut Block
Garnish: Blood Orange Twist & Pine Sprig
Glass: Tumbler

METHOD
—
Add all the ingredients to a shaker with ice & shake

Roll your shaker from side to side in a slow motion
a couple of times

Strain into a tumbler & add ice

Garnish with a blood orange twist & a sprig of pine

GREEN YARD

GROVE 42 · LEMON · BASIL · MATCHA

—

ERIK LORINCZ – AMERICAN BAR AT THE SAVOY, LONDON

Best Bar in the World – World's 50 Best Bar Awards 2017

INGREDIENTS

—

Grove 42: 2 oz
Fresh Lemon Juice: 2 tbsp
Sugar Syrup (*see page 186*): 1 tbsp
Basil Leaf: 1
Cardamom Droplets (*see page 184*): 3
Egg White: 1
Ice: Cubed
Garnish: Matcha Powder (*see page 185*)
Glass: Coupe

METHOD

—

Add all the ingredients, except the ice,
to a jug & blend with a hand blender

Tip into a shaker with the ice & shake

Double strain into a coupe glass

Garnish with a sprinkle of matcha powder

CARROT CORDIAL
MAKES 2 CUPS

—

INGREDIENTS
Water: 2 cups
Superfine Sugar: 2 ½ cups
Carrot Peelings: 9 oz

METHOD
Add all the ingredients to a saucepan
over medium heat & bring to a boil.
Reduce the heat, cover & simmer for
30 minutes. Remove from the heat,
cool & strain into a bottle.
Keeps refrigerated for 1 month

MALT SYRUP
MAKES APPROX. 2 CUPS

—

INGREDIENTS
Water: 1 cup
Superfine Sugar: 1 ¼ cups
Cacao: ¾ oz
Toasted Unmalted Barley: 1 ½ oz

METHOD
Add the water to a saucepan & bring
to a boil. Add the sugar, stirring until it
dissolves. Remove from the heat & leave
to cool. Add the cacao & barley & stir.
Leave for 30 minutes. Strain & bottle.
Keeps for 1 month

BONFIRE GLYNCTURE
MAKES APPROX. 1 CUP

—

INGREDIENTS
Manuka Bark (*see page 185*): ⅓ oz
Lapsang Souchong Tea: 1 ¾ oz
Timut Pepper (*see page 187*): 1 oz
Vegetable Glycerine (*see page 187*): ¾ cup
Water: ⅓ cup

METHOD
Mix the manuka bark, tea & pepper
in a Mason jar. Add the vegetable glycerine
& water & leave for 2 days. Strain & bottle.
Keeps for 6 months

SUNSHINE SYRUP
MAKES 1 CUP

—

INGREDIENTS
Orange: 1
Lemon: 1
Grapefruit: 1
Superfine Sugar: 2 ½ cups
Water: 1 cup

METHOD
Zest the orange, lemon & grapefruit
& add to a saucepan over medium
heat with the other ingredients & bring
to a boil. Reduce the heat & simmer
for 30 minutes. Strain & leave to cool.
Bottle.
Keeps for 1 month

CASCARA SYRUP

MAKES 1 ²/₃ CUPS

—

INGREDIENTS

Superfine Sugar: 1 ¼ cups
Water: 1 cup
Cascara (*see page 184*): 4 oz

METHOD

Add the sugar, water & cascara to a
saucepan over medium heat & bring
to a boil. Stir until the sugar dissolves
Remove from the heat & leave to cool.
Strain & bottle.
Keeps refrigerated for 1 month

YUZU VERJUS

MAKES ½ CUP

—

INGREDIENTS

Yuzu Juice (*see page 187*): 2 tsp
Sugar Syrup (*see page 186*): 2 tsp
Verjus (White Grape Juice): 6 ½ tbsp

METHOD

Add the yuzu juice, sugar syrup
& verjus to a bottle & shake.
Keeps for 1 week

MANGO DROPS

MAKES 1 ¼ CUPS

—

INGREDIENTS

Mango: 1
Vegetable Glycerine (*see page 187*): ¾
cup
Water: ⅓–½ cup

METHOD

Dice the mango & add to a Mason jar.
Pour in the vegetable glycerine & water.
Leave for 48 hours in the fridge.
Strain & bottle.
Keeps for 1 month

ROOIBOS & TURMERIC CORDIAL

MAKES APPROX. 1 ²/₃ CUPS

—

INGREDIENTS

Rooibos Tea: ¾ oz
Ground Turmeric: Pinch
Superfine Sugar: 2 ½ cups
Hot Water: 1 cup

METHOD

Add the ingredients to a bowl & stir well.
Leave to infuse until cold.
Strain & bottle.
Keeps refrigerated for 1 week

GORSE & BEESWAX SHRUB

MAKES 1 CUP

—

INGREDIENTS

Gorse Flowers: 8 oz
Beeswax: ⅓ oz
Lincolnshire Honey: 1 cup
Raw Apple Vinegar: ¼ cup

METHOD

Add all the ingredients to a bowl & mix together. Sous vide (*see page 186*) at 125°F for 6 hours. Fine strain & bottle.
Keeps refrigerated for 1 month

VANILLA PEANUT MILK

MAKES 2 CUPS

—

INGREDIENTS

Unsalted Peanuts: 1 ⅓ cups
Water: 1 ⅔ cups
Vanilla Pod: ½

METHOD

Preheat the oven to 325°F.
Place the peanuts on a baking sheet & roast until golden & smelling delicious. Soak in water overnight (this makes them easier to blitz). Tip the peanuts & water into a blender. Scrape the seeds from the vanilla pod & add to the peanuts. Blend until smooth. Pass through a super bag (*see page 186*), then bottle.
Keeps refrigerated for 3 days

ROSEMARY DUST

MAKES 1 TBSP

—

INGREDIENTS

Rosemary Sprig: 1
Sugar Syrup (*see page 186*): ¾ oz
Salt: Pinch
Matcha Powder (*see page 185*): ¼ tsp

METHOD

Dip the rosemary sprig in the sugar syrup, then sprinkle with salt. Dehydrate overnight in a dehydrator or in an oven set to a low temperature. When brittle, grind in a mortar & pestle. Sieve to get a fine powder. Add matcha powder.
Keeps in an airtight container for 6 months

CARDAMOM SYRUP

MAKES 1 ½ CUPS

—

INGREDIENTS

Water: 1 cup
Cardamom Pods: 2 oz
Superfine Sugar: 2 ½ cups

METHOD

Add the water and cardamom to a saucepan over medium heat & bring to a boil. Stir in the sugar until fully dissolved. Reduce the heat, cover with a lid & simmer for about 15 minutes. Remove from the heat and allow to cool. Leave to infuse in the refrigerator for 3 days, then strain & bottle.
Keeps refrigerated for 3 weeks

PINE-SMOKED BLOOD ORANGE JUICE

MAKES APPROX. ¾ CUP

—

INGREDIENTS

Blood Oranges: 6
Pine Branches: 3

METHOD

Cut the oranges in half & place in a
smoker with the pine branches. Smoke
for at least 30 minutes. (If you don't have
a smoker, a smoking gun can be used
to bubble smoke through the juice
of the oranges – use pine needles
in the smoking gun). Juice the
orange halves & bottle.
Keeps refrigerated for 1 week

PINE CORDIAL

MAKES ¾ CUP

—

INGREDIENTS

Pine: 5 finger-sized sprigs
Water: ¾ cup
Superfine Sugar: about ½ cup
Citric Acid: Pinch

METHOD

Add the pine & water to a saucepan
& heat until almost boiling. Reduce
the heat & simmer for 10–15 minutes.
Remove from the heat & strain; add
the equivalent weight in sugar to the
remaining water & stir to dissolve.
Stir in the citric acid & leave
to cool. Bottle.
Keeps for 1 month

SPICED GRILLED PLUM PURÉE

MAKES APPROX. ¾ CUP

—

INGREDIENTS

Plums: 6
Cloves: 6
Ground Ginger: 1 tsp
Ground Star Anise: ½ tsp
Water: ⅓–½ cup
Molasses Sugar: ⅓–½ cup (depending
on the sharpness of the plums)

METHOD

Halve & pit the plums.
Put a griddle pan over a high heat &,
once hot, add the plums, flesh side down.
Add the cloves, ginger & star anise.
When the plums start to blacken, cover
the pan with foil & turn off the heat.
Leave to smoke & steam for a few
minutes. Remove from the heat & put the
plums & spices in a blender.
Add the water & molasses sugar & blend
until puréed. Pass through a fine sieve.
Leave to cool, then store in a Mason jar.
Keeps refrigerated for 2 weeks

SHRUBS & SYRUPS

With a little bit of preparation & planning you can make some
wonderful long & refreshing Seedlip Sodas. It's a great way to
experiment, use up leftovers & make the most of the ingredients
lurking in your kitchen cabinet. The basic recipe is:

SEEDLIP
+
SHRUB OR SYRUP
+
SODA

The following pages are recipes from various members of the
Seedlip Team using shrubs & syrups to make tasty Seedlip Sodas.

SHRUBS

Shrubs have their origins in 17th-century England, when vinegar was used as an alternative to citrus to preserve the glut of fruits & vegetables for the off-season. Vinegar's acidic preserving properties are perfect for storing a shrub for a month in the fridge & the options are truly endless. Our shrubs are made based on this simple formula:

PLANT + VINEGAR + SUGAR + TIME = SHRUB

SYRUPS

Syrups use sugar to carry flavor. More concentrated than a cordial, a little syrup can go a very long way. Syrups, when made well, keep well. Stored in the fridge, a syrup made with 1 part sugar to 1 part water should last 1 month, while a syrup made with 2 parts sugar to 1 part water should last 6 months because it's more concentrated.

PLANT + SUGAR + WATER + HEAT = SYRUP

SPICE 94
SHRUBS

SPICED BEETROOT SHRUB
KAITLIN WILKES – LONDON
MAKES 1 ½ CUPS

—

INGREDIENTS
Cooked Beets: 4
Superfine Sugar: 1 ¼ cups
Cinnamon Sticks: 2
Cardamom Pods: 6
Black Peppercorns: 1 tsp
Cloves: 6
Apple Cider Vinegar: ⅓–½ cup

METHOD
Chop the beets into small pieces
& place in a bowl with the sugar.
Fry the spices in a dry pan over
a medium heat until lightly toasted
& releasing an aroma. Add the toasted
spices to the beets & sugar & leave
to sit overnight (for a minimum of
12 hours – the longer, the better!).
Stir the sugar, beets & spices together
& leave for another 3–5 hours.
Pass through a sieve to remove the
spices & beets (but keep the beets aside
for garnish). Add the vinegar
to the sugar & stir, then bottle.
Keeps refrigerated for 2 months

SPICED BEETROOT
COCKTAIL

—

INGREDIENTS
Spice 94: 2 oz
Spiced Beetroot Shrub: 1 ½ oz
Soda: Top
Ice: Cubed
Garnish: Leftover Beet
Glass: Tall

METHOD
Add the Spice 94 & Spiced Beetroot
Shrub to a tall glass. Add ice & stir
quickly. Top with soda.
Garnish with beet.

GOLDEN HOUR SHRUB

SARAH PARNIAK – TORONTO
MAKES APPROX. 2 CUPS

INGREDIENTS

Anjou Pear (*see page 184*): 1 lb
Minced Jamaican Ginger
(*see page 185*): 1 tsp
Apple Cider Vinegar: 1 cup
Sugar Syrup (*see page 186*): 1 cup
Saffron Threads: 8

METHOD

Dice the pears & add to a Mason jar
with the ginger, vinegar, sugar syrup
& saffron & muddle. Leave for 36 hours.
Strain through cheesecloth into
another jar.
Keeps refrigerated for 1 month

GOLDEN HOUR COCKTAIL

INGREDIENTS

Spice 94: 2 oz
Golden Hour Shrub: 1 oz
Soda: 2 ½ oz
Ice: Cubed
Garnish: Sage Leaf
Glass: Tall

METHOD

Add the Spice 94 & Golden Hour Shrub
to a tall glass over ice. Top with soda.
Garnish with a sage leaf.

K-TOWN SHRUB

AARON POLSKY – LA
MAKES APPROX. 1 QUART

INGREDIENTS

Water: 1 ¾ cups
Superfine Sugar: 2 ¼ cups
Asian Pear: 4 oz
Fresh Root Ginger: 4 oz
Persimmon Vinegar: ⅓–½ cup
Gochugaru Chile Flakes
(*see page 185*): 1 oz

METHOD

Combine the water & sugar in a bowl.
Stir until dissolved. Finely slice the pear
& ginger & add to the sugar water with
the rest of the ingredients. Leave to
infuse in a refrigerator for 24 hours.
Strain & bottle.
Keeps refrigerated for 1 month

K-TOWN COCKTAIL

INGREDIENTS

Spice 94: 2 oz
K-Town Shrub: ¾ oz
Fresh Lemon Juice: ¾ oz
Soda: Top
Ice: Cubed
Garnish: Tangerine Segment
Glass: Tall

METHOD

Add the Spice 94, K-Town Shrub &
lemon juice to a shaker & shake. Strain
into a tall glass with ice. Top with soda.
Garnish with a tangerine segment.

GARDEN 108
SHRUBS

PERSEPHONE SHRUB
JAMES SNELGROVE – SYDNEY
MAKES APPROX. 5 CUPS

—

INGREDIENTS
Cassia Quills (*see page 184*): 2
Toasted Walnuts: ¼ cup
Persimmon: 1 lb
Superfine Sugar: 2 ½ cups
Sea Salt: ½ tsp
Apple Cider Vinegar: ¾ cup

METHOD
Fry the cassia & walnuts in a dry pan
over medium heat until lightly toasted &
releasing an aroma. Slice the persimmon
into ⅜-inch cubes. Place the toasted
cassia & walnuts into an airtight
container with the persimmon sugar &
salt. Leave at room temperature
out of direct sunlight for 3 days.
Pass through a sieve to remove the
solids. Add the vinegar & stir. Bottle.
Keeps refrigerated for 3 weeks

PERSEPHONE COCKTAIL
—

INGREDIENTS
Garden 108: 2 oz
Persephone Shrub: 1 oz
Ice: Cubed
Garnish: Persimmon Wheel &
Grated Toasted Walnut
Glass: Tall

METHOD
Place the Garden 108 & Persephone
Shrub in a tall glass. Top with soda.
Garnish with a persimmon wheel
& grated toasted walnut.

LAWN GAMES SHRUB
LAURA LASHLEY – LA
MAKES APPROX. 3 ¼ CUPS

—

INGREDIENTS
Blueberries: 2 ¼ lb
Dried Lemon Myrtle (*see page 185*):
¼ cup
White Wine Vinegar: 2 cups
Superfine Sugar: 2 ½ cups

METHOD
Add the blueberries, lemon
myrtle, vinegar & sugar to a Mason
jar & muddle. Leave for 3 days.
Gently press the berries
to extract the juice.
Fine strain & bottle.
Keeps refrigerated for 1 month

LAWN GAMES COCKTAIL

—

INGREDIENTS
Garden 108: 2 oz
Lawn Games Shrub: 1 oz
Fresh Lemon Juice: Dash
Soda: Top
Ice: Cubed
Garnish: Lemon Wheel
Glass: Tall

METHOD
Add the Garden 108, Lawn Games
Shrub & lemon juice to a tall glass
with ice & stir. Top with soda. Garnish
with a lemon wheel.

SUMMER SOMEWHERE
JASMIN RUTTER – AUCKLAND
MAKES 2 CUPS

—

INGREDIENTS
Pineapple Skins: 1
Hops Pellets: 4
Thyme Sprigs: 8
Apple Cider Vinegar: ¾ cup
Superfine Sugar: 2 ½ cups
Water: ⅓–½ cup

METHOD
Add the skin from 1 pineapple
& the hops, thyme, vinegar & sugar
to a Mason jar & gently shake. Leave
for 48 hours. Strain through cheesecloth.
Add the water & bottle.
Keeps refrigerated for 2 weeks

SUMMER SOMEWHERE
COCKTAIL

—

INGREDIENTS
Garden 108: 2 oz
Summer Somewhere Shrub: 1 oz
Soda: Top
Ice: Cubed
Garnish: Thyme
Glass: Tall

METHOD
Pour the Garden 108 & Summer
Somewhere Shrub into a tall glass
with ice. Top with soda.
Garnish with a sprig of thyme.

SPICE 94
SYRUPS

TEA IN THE AFTERNOON SYRUP

LAURA LASHLEY – LA
MAKES 1 QUART

—

INGREDIENTS
Superfine Sugar: 2 ½ cups
Water: 2 cups
Orange Peel: 1
Lemon Peel: 1
Earl Grey Tea: 5 tbsp
Lavender Flowers: 2 tbsp

METHOD
Add the sugar, water & peels of
the orange & lemon to a saucepan
& bring to a boil. Reduce the heat
& simmer for 10–15 minutes.
Add the tea & lavender flowers
& simmer for a further 3–5 minutes.
Fine strain & leave to cool.
Keeps refrigerated for 1 month

TEA IN THE AFTERNOON COCKTAIL

—

INGREDIENTS
Spice 94: 2 oz
Tea in the Afternoon Syrup: ¾ oz
Fresh Lemon Juice: 2 tsp
Soda: Top
Garnish: Orange Twist
Glass: Tall

METHOD
Add the Spice 94, Tea in the
Afternoon Syrup & lemon juice to
a tall glass with ice. Top with soda.
Garnish with an orange twist.

TEA & TOAST SYRUP – BREAKFAST COLLINS
CLAIRE WARNER – LONDON
MAKES APPROX. 2 CUPS

—

INGREDIENTS
Lightly Burnt Sourdough: 4 oz
Muscovado Sugar: 1/3 cup
Sea Salt: Pinch
Hot Strong Black Tea: 2 cups

METHOD
Place the sourdough, sugar & salt in
a food processor & blend to bread crumbs.
Add the hot black tea & stir. Leave to
infuse for 10 minutes. Fine
strain & chill.
Keeps refrigerated for 3 weeks

BREAKFAST COLLINS COCKTAIL

—

INGREDIENTS
Spice 94: 2 oz
Tea & Toast Syrup: 1 oz
Fresh Lemon Juice: Dash
Soda: Top
Ice: Cubed
Garnish: Lemon Wheel
Glass: Tumbler

METHOD
Add the Spice 94, Tea & Toast
Syrup & lemon juice to a tumbler
over ice. Top with soda.
Garnish with a lemon wheel.

SAGE AGAINST THE MACHINE
SEBASTIAN ROBINSON – HONG KONG
MAKES APPROX. 2 CUPS

—

INGREDIENTS
Sage Leaves: 1/4 cup
Blueberries: 4 oz
Superfine Sugar: about 1 cup
Water: 1 cup
Star Anise: 4

METHOD
Add the sage, blueberries, sugar &
water to a saucepan & bring to a boil.
Reduce the heat & simmer gently until
the sugar has dissolved. Muddle the
blueberries to release the juice. Add the
star anise, remove from the heat & leave
to cool. Fine strain into a glass bottle.
Keeps refrigerated for 1 month

SAGE AGAINST THE MACHINE COCKTAIL

—

INGREDIENTS
Spice 94: 2 oz
Sage Against the Machine Syrup:
3/4 oz
Soda: Top
Ice: Cubed
Garnish: Candied Sage leaf
Glass: Tall

METHOD
Add the Spice 94 & Sage Against
the Machine Syrup to a tall glass
with ice. Top with soda.
Garnish with a candied sage leaf.

GARDEN 108
SYRUPS

PROUD MARY SYRUP

NORA FURST – SAN FRANCISCO

MAKES 1 ²/₃ CUPS

—

INGREDIENTS

Tomato Scraps: 4 oz
Beet Scraps: 4 oz
Lemon Skins: 3 (from 1 ½ lemons)
Dill: 1 ½ oz
Water: 2 cups
Superfine Sugar: ½ cup
Kosher Salt: 1 tsp
Citric Acid: ¼ tsp

METHOD

Rinse & thoroughly scrub all scraps
& skins. Add the dill, tomatoes & beets to
a saucepan over medium heat, cover with
the water & bring to a boil. Boil for
10 minutes, or until the tomatoes begin to
break down. Add the lemon skins
& boil for another 3–4 minutes. Remove
the lemon skins with tongs & fine strain.
Press the veggies with the back of a
wooden spoon to squeeze out all liquid.
Pass the liquid through a fine strainer to
clarify. Whisk in the sugar, salt & citric acid
until they dissolve. Leave to cool & bottle.

Keeps for 1 month

PROUD MARY
COCKTAIL

—

INGREDIENTS

Garden 108: 2 oz
Proud Mary Syrup: 1 oz
Soda: Top
Ice: Cubed
Garnish: Dill
Glass: Tall

METHOD

Add the Garden 108 & Proud
Mary Syrup to a tall glass with ice.
Top with soda.
Garnish with a sprig of dill.

DOWN THE GARDEN PATH SYRUP

SARAH PARNIAK

MAKES 2 CUPS

———

INGREDIENTS

Rhubarb: 1 lb
Tarragon Sprig: 1
Water: 1 cup
Superfine Sugar: 1 ¼ cups
Sea Salt: Pinch

METHOD

Dice the rhubarb & add to a saucepan over medium heat with the tarragon & water & bring to a boil. Reduce the heat & simmer gently for 10 minutes. Add the sugar & salt & stir to dissolve. Strain into a bottle & leave to cool.
Keeps refrigerated for 1 month

DOWN THE GARDEN PATH COCKTAIL

———

INGREDIENTS

Garden 108: 2 oz
Down the Garden Path Syrup: 1 oz
Soda: Top
Ice: Cubed
Garnish: Tarragon
Glass: Chilled Tall

METHOD

Add the Garden 108 & Down the Garden Path Syrup to a shaker with ice & shake. Strain into a chilled tall glass. Top with soda. Garnish with a sprig of tarragon.

MELLOW YELLOW SYRUP

KAITLIN WILKES – LONDON

MAKES 1 ⅔ CUPS

———

INGREDIENTS

Large Cooking Apples: 4
Superfine Sugar: 1 ¼ cups
Rosemary Sprigs: 3

METHOD

Peel 2 apples & cut the flesh into small ⅜-inch cubes. Tip into a bowl & cover with the sugar & rosemary. Leave overnight. Juice the remaining 2 apples & add it to the bowl. Leave to rest at room temperature for a further night. On the third day, make sure most of the sugar has dissolved, then strain into a bottle.
Keeps for 1 month

MELLOW YELLOW COCKTAIL

———

INGREDIENTS

Garden 108: 2 oz
Mellow Yellow Syrup: 1 oz
Soda: Top
Ice: Cubed
Garnish: Rosemary
Glass: Tall

METHOD

Add the Garden 108 & Mellow Yellow Syrup to a tall glass with ice. Top with soda. Garnish with a sprig of rosemary.

GROVE 42
SYRUPS

A LONG HARVEST SYRUP
STEWART HOWARD – LONDON
MAKES 2 ½ CUPS

—

INGREDIENTS
Barley: 4 oz
Large Figs: 4
Superfine Sugar: 2 cups
Boiling Water: ¾ cup

METHOD
Dry-fry the barley in a pan over medium
heat until toasted & lightly brown. Mash
the figs & add them to the barley. Add the
sugar to the boiling water in a saucepan
& stir to dissolve. Combine all the
ingredients together
& vacuum pack (*see page 187*) for
24 hours. Double strain & bottle.
Keeps refrigerated for 3 months

A LONG HARVEST
COCKTAIL

INGREDIENTS
Grove 42: 2 oz
A Long Harvest Syrup: 1 tbsp
Soda: Top
Ice: Cubed
Garnish: Barley
Glass: Tumbler

METHOD
Add the Grove 42 & A Long
Harvest Syrup to a tumbler over ice.
Top with soda.
Garnish with a sprig of barley.

VENETIAN LEAF SYRUP
LUKE PEARSON – BIRMINGHAM
MAKES 1 QUART

—

INGREDIENTS
Hot Water: 2 cups
Olive Leaf Tea: 1 ½ tbsp
Jasmine Sencha (*see page 185*): 1 tbsp
Superfine Sugar: 2 ½ cups

METHOD
Place the water in a saucepan and
heat to 176°C. Add the olive leaf tea
& jasmine sencha & infuse for
15 minutes. Strain into another
pan & add the sugar. Stir to dissolve, then
bottle.
Keeps refrigerated for 2 weeks

VENETIAN LEAF COCKTAIL
—

INGREDIENTS
Grove 42: 2 oz
Venetian Leaf Syrup: 1 tbsp
Soda: Top
Ice: Cubed
Garnish: Orange Wedge & Olive
Glass: Wine

METHOD
Add the Grove 42 & Venetian
Leaf Syrup to a wineglass over ice.
Top with soda. Garnish with an
orange wedge & an olive.

BEACH SYRUP
BEN BRANSON – OLD AMERSHAM
MAKES ENOUGH FOR 4 ICE POPS

—

INGREDIENTS
Sea Salt: 2 pinches
Waffle Cones: 3
Vanilla Syrup: 2 tsp
Superfine Sugar: 1 ¼ cups
Water: 1 cup
Orange Natural Food Coloring:
3 drops
Fresh Orange Juice: 2 tsp

METHOD
Add all the ingredients to a saucepan
over medium heat. Stir to dissolve.
Strain, leave to cool & bottle.
Keeps for 1 month

BEACH LOLLY
—

INGREDIENTS
Grove 42: 1 oz
Beach Syrup: 1 tbsp
Soda: 1 oz
Garnish: Sunshine
Glass: Ice Pop Mold

METHOD
Mix the Grove 42, Beach Syrup
& soda in a glass & stir. Pour
into 4 ice pop molds & freeze.
Keeps frozen for 3 months

GLOSSARY
OF INGREDIENTS & TECHNIQUES

Aquafaba: The viscous liquid in which legume seeds, such as chickpeas, have been cooked. Due to having similar functional properties to egg whites, aquafaba can be used as an egg white replacement in some cases – a dairy-free option for sours.

Bitter Syrup: Fabri Bitter Syrup is a rich red, bitter syrup that's not the easiest to find but worth the search online. Monin Bitter Syrup is a rich red, bittersweet syrup.

Cascara: Meaning "husk" or "peel," cascara is the outer skin & pulp of a coffee cherry. It has a subtle sweetness & can be used to make sodas & syrups.

Cassia: Sometimes referred to as "Chinese cinnamon," cassia is the aromatic bark of an East Asian tree, similar in taste to cinnamon.

Celery Seed Salt Solution: Add 2–3 tbsp celery salt (equal parts celery seed & sea salt) to ¾ cup boiling water, stir & cool.

Centrifuge: A machine with a compartment that rotates at speed, using centrifugal force to separate liquids of different densities.

Champagne Vinegar: Made from the same grapes as Champagne, this is a mild-tasting, dry white wine vinegar. Although not directly made from Champagne itself, it has to come from the Champagne region in France.

Chinois: A cone-shaped sieve with very fine mesh. Used for straining liquids or dusting fine-powdered ingredients.

Chitosan: A natural fiber product, derived from chitin, which is a substance found in the exoskeleton of shellfish, such as lobster.

Circulator/Immersion Circulator: An electrical device that heats & circulates warm fluids & maintains a selected temperature, using the sous vide (*see page 186*) method.

D'Anjou Pear: A squat, egg-shaped pear that is particularly sweet & juicy.

D'Anjou Pear Vinegar: From the d'Anjou pear, this vinegar is light in color & has an aromatic pear flavor.

Double Strain: Use a cocktail strainer & fine tea strainer.

Droplets: We recommend Javier de las Muelas' range of nonalcoholic flavors: shop.javierdelasmuelas.com/thedryshop/en/

Erdinger Nonalcoholic Beer: There are quite a few nonalcoholic beers available now – Erdinger's has had some great reviews.

Fee Bros Nonalcoholic Aromatic Bitters: You can buy these online & they are great additions to cocktails. They are vegetable-glycerine-based extracts that are highly concentrated & come in a range of flavors.

Fine Strain: Use a fine gauze to sift out unwanted material. Available from all good homeware stores.

Fuyu Persimmon: Native to Asia, this fruit can be eaten raw, dried or cooked & has a rich sweetness. The fruit looks similar to an orange tomato, although it is categorized as a berry.

Gochugaru Chile Flakes: These chile flakes have smoky, fruity & sweet notes & originate from Korea. The flakes are an essential ingredient in kimchi & are used to give it a hot kick.

Heavy-Steeped Tea: A good hour of steeping will give you a rich tea.

Honey Syrup: Made from equal quantities of honey & water – the honey is added to hot water & dissolved.

Ice: There are 3 basic kinds – cubed (regular cubed ice); hand-cut block ice (a large block of ice cut to bigger cubes or columns); & crushed/pebble ice (small crushed ice).

Jamaican Ginger: Regarded as a premium variety of ginger, it is characterized by a pale-yellow inside & off-white skin. It is more aromatic than other varieties of ginger.

Jasmine Sencha: A medium-bodied tea, jasmine adds floral notes to the grassy, traditional Japanese sencha tea.

Kieselsol: A fining agent made from silicon dioxide & used for clarifying liquids. Other fining agents are gelatin, pectinase & activated charcoal.

Lemon & Ginger Juice: Either buy lemon juice & ginger juice & combine, or juice a lemon & fresh root ginger & combine.

Lemon Myrtle: A shrub native to the rainforests of Australia. Its leaves, when dried & crushed, add an intense lemon flavor to dishes.

Lemongrass Kombucha: A tart & refreshing sparkling drink made from fermented tea. We recommend the one from our friends at LA Brewery.

Lemon Pelargonium Leaves: Lemon pelargonium is a herb with felt-like leaves that hold a lemon flavor & can be infused into drinks to inject citrus notes.

Malic Acid: One of the main fruit acids. Naturally occurring in apples & berries, malic acid has a tart flavor & can be found in most health food shops in powdered form.

Manuka Bark: From the manuka tree, native to New Zealand. The bark is stringy & peels in long flakes. Often used in teas & for medicinal purposes, it was made famous by the honey of the same name.

Matcha Powder: A high-quality, powdered green tea from Japan. It is finely powdered & consists of only the nutrient-rich young leaves picked from the tips of *Camellia sinensis* plants.

Microplane: A fine grater, used for zesting citrus fruits & grating nutmeg.

Mixing Glass: A piece of cocktail-making equipment used to stir & chill drinks before they are strained into the glass.

Oak Smoke Droplets: These droplets are used to add a wood-smoked, resin flavor to food & beverages. We recommend Javier de las Muelas' Droplets.

Orange Blossom Water: A flavoring distilled from

blossoms of the orange tree. It has a soapy aroma & taste & is excellent in food & drink in small quantities.

Pectinex Ultra SP-L: An enzyme that breaks down pectin structure. It is also an aid when clarifying juices.

Pink Peppercorn Gum Syrup: Add equal weights of pink peppercorns & sugar & water to a saucepan. Heat gently, stirring until the sugar has dissolved, then steep for 1 hour. Strain & store. Keeps for 3 months.

Powdered Kola Nut: This bitter-tasting powder is made from the nuts of the kola tree (native to Africa). It has been used as a flavoring agent in soda drinks for many years. It is the origin of the term "cola."

PS Lemon Myrtle Soda: Our friends at PS40 Bar in Sydney make this delicious "Bush Tonic" with Peruvian cinchona bark, lemon & lime zest, lemongrass & lemon myrtle.

Pu'erh Tea: A variety of fermented tea produced in Yannun, China. The more

aged the tea, the more earthy the aroma.

Rhubarb Soda: An intense, earthy drink. We recommend Square Root Soda, or juicing rhubarb & adding soda to make your own.

Rich Sugar Syrup: Similar to a sugar syrup, but with 2 parts sugar to 1 part water.
Royal Flush Real Kombucha: Kombucha is fermented tea & our friends at Real make a delicious Darjeeling-based "booch."

Sandows Cold Brew Concentrate: Coffee beans steeped cold & filtered. Friends of ours at Sandows make the best cold-brew coffee.

Shiso Leaf: Belonging to the mint family, this herb has a unique herbaceous & citrusy taste. There are green- & purple-leaved varieties, with a jagged shape & slightly prickly texture.

Sorrel Juice: Made from the petals of the sorrel plant, this juice is dark in color & has a sour raspberry-like flavor.
Sugar Syrup: This is the simplest of sugar syrups, made

with equal weights of sugar & water.

Smoker: An appliance used to infuse food or drink with smoky flavors without using heat.

Sous Vide: A heating method in which food is placed in a plastic pouch & immersed in water with a regulated temperature over a long period of time. This allows the food to cook evenly throughout while maintaining moisture.

Spindle Mix: An appliance used to speed up cocktail making. It can be used to pulse or flash-mix cocktails.

Super Bag: A very fine filter in the form of a flexible sieve. |Used to strain sediment out of liquids, it can withstand high temperatures & is reusable.

Sweet & Dandy: The name of a brand of mauby syrup, which is a Caribbean drink made from mauby bark. It adds a sweet ice cream flavor to drinks & has a clove aftertaste.

Tartaric Acid: An organic substance occurring naturally

in many plants & fruits, most notably in grapes, it is sour in flavor & is used as an additive to inject a sharp, tart flavor to food or drinks.

Timut Pepper: Originating from Nepal, this is a rare peppercorn with a vibrant aroma of passion fruit & grapefruit. When eaten, it leaves a tingling sensation in your mouth for a few minutes.

Tincture: Alcohol extracts from herbs & plants in a solution, often used for medicinal purposes.

Tonka Bean Droplets: The tonka bean is the flat, dark, wrinkled seed from giant cumaru trees in South America. These fragrant droplets inject a complex sour cherry, clove and cinnamon taste to cocktails. We recommend Javier de las Muelas' Droplets, which are glycerine-based, nonalcoholic flavors.

Top: A quantity of carbonated liquid, roughly equivalent to 1/3 cup, used in cocktail making to finish the drink.

Twist & Sparkle Bottle: Used to carbonate alcoholic & nonalcoholic drinks using a plastic operating element fueled by a carbon dioxide charger, it adds carbonation directly into the drink.

Vacuum Pack: A method of packaging that removes air from inside the package before sealing, thus removing oxygen & extending shelf life.

Vanilla Peanut Milk: Add 8 oz unsalted, roasted peanuts to 2 cups water & soak for 6 hours. Place the peanuts, 3 ¼ cups water, 2 dates & ½ tsp vanilla extract into a blender & blend for 1 minute. Strain using cheesecloth.

Vegetable Glycerine: A clear liquid produced from plant oils. Often used as a replacement for alcohol in herbal & botanical tinctures, it adds sweetness to drinks.

Wattleseed: A nutritious roasted seed from the acacia shrub, originating in Australia. The distinctive coffee, chocolate & hazelnut flavor means wattleseed can be used in both savory & sweet dishes.

Yuzu: A citrus fruit from Japan with a distinct sourness & taste similar to grapefruit & lime mixed together. The yuzu is the size of a tangerine & is used for its juice & aromatic rind.

INDEX